Collins

Computer World 5

Series Editor
Mohini Arora

Published by Collins India
A division of HarperCollins*Publishers* India Limited
A-75, Sector-57,
Noida-201301

Browse the complete Collins catalogue at **www.collins.in**

First edition 2015

Reprint: 10 9 8 7 6 5 4 3 2 1

ISBN: 978-93-5136-650-8

Content developed by **Srimon Chatterjee**

Artwork and layout by **AptaraCorp Ltd.**

Printed and bound by **Thomson Press (India) Limited**

Acknowledgements

Cover: Sashkin

Title Page: Sashkin

Preface

Computer World, a series of eight books for Classes 1 to 8, is an effort to familiarize and equip students with the latest trends in computer technology. This is a well-graded course that conforms to the requirements of National Curriculum Framework (2005) and complies with the syllabus requirements of various boards.

The course is based on **Windows 7** and **MS Office 2010** with updates on Windows 8 and MS Office 2013. The progression of the series ensures that the pedagogical needs of the students are met.

The course introduces computers in the primary classes in a simple and lucid manner. It strengthens programming concepts and gives students an opportunity to explore and experiment with the latest software in higher classes. The series has the latest versions namely, MS Visual Basic 2010 Express, Windows Movie Maker 2012, HTML 5, Adobe Dreamweaver CC, Adobe Photoshop CC and Adobe Flash 8.

The course is a perfect blend of theoretical and practical topics, and is interspersed with illustrations, keyboard shortcuts and facts. The language used for explanation is simple and the content is supported by step-by-step explanations and well-labeled screenshots.

Sections like You Should Know, Quick Way, Quick Recap, Word Web and Teacher's Notes cover and recapitulate the concepts through each dimension. A detailed overview of the key features of the books is given in the **Key Features** spread on the next two pages.

To enable the students face the challenges and to provide them a competitive edge by developing their lateral thinking and analytical skills, following sections are given in each book:

- Worksheets and Projects
- Assessments
- Revision Questions
- National Cyber Olympiad by Science Olympiad Foundation–for Classes 3 to 8

To meet all the learning objectives and to provide a holistic form of imparting education, the questions in various sections are based on the **Bloom's Taxonomy**. This ensures that the concept understanding is tested at six different levels, namely Knowledge, Comprehension, Application, Analysis, Synthesis and Evaluation.

Lab Activities and Research Projects are given with the aim of inducing curiosity and familiarizing the students with practical applications of the topics. All the books in this series have relevant sections flagged with FA and SA icons, indicating that these sections can be considered as formative and summative assessments.

Collins DigiSuite is an interactive digital solution which provides an e-book with learning materials and interactive teaching tools that will help the teachers to prepare additional notes and practice questions for students.

I would like to thank all the teachers who have reviewed the series and the publisher who has invested its resources in bringing out this course to inspire the learners today. I sincerely welcome constructive feedback and suggestions to improve these books further in subsequent editions.

Authors

Key Features

You Should Know

When we cut or copy a portion of text, Windows stores that portion in a temporary storage area called the **Clipboard**.

feature includes interesting facts about the topic

Quick Way

To open a new presentation in PowerPoint, press the **Control** key (**Ctrl** key) and the letter **N** together.

feature highlights all the important keyboard shortcuts for the menu commands

Word Web

Malicious: harmful and destructive

gives the meaning of all the difficult words

Practice Time 2

Use the commands to draw and write the following in MSWLogo.

1. Each side of the square is 100 units

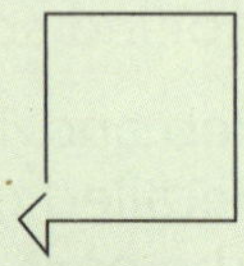

to provide solution to hands-on practice questions given after covering important concepts

WINDOWS 8

UPDATES

Windows 8 is an improved version of the Windows 7 operating system. It provides all of the basic features that Windows 7 has. The focus of Windows 8 is on optimizing the operating system for touchscreen-based devices (such as tablets) and cloud computing.

Unlike Windows Vista and Windows 7, there are no Starter, Home Basic, Home Premium or Ultimate editions in Windows 8. The most common editions of Windows 8 are Windows 8 Pro and Windows 8 Enterprise.

section has updates on Windows 8 and MS Office 2013 for Classes 3 to 8

Quick Recap

1. Internet is a vast computer network which connects millions of computers all over the world with one another and makes information sharing between these machines possible.
2. Internet Explorer 11 is the latest web browser from Microsoft.

recapitulates all the important points covered in the chapter

Teacher's Notes

Discussion Ideas:

- Discuss various elements covered in this chapter and their attributes.

Demonstrations

- Demonstrate the effect of all the values of the align attribute of the <p> element.

contains interesting topic-related notes that teachers can take up in class and demonstrate to students

Research Project

FA

Vivek has collected about 20 pictures of his school and wants to share these pictures with his friends. Which program should he use for doing this?

is integrated with all the subjects and is aimed at testing the students' application skills

Lab Activity

Try the following in your computer lab.

1. Your class teacher has asked you to prepare a list of the students in your class along with their roll numbers and marks in a class test in MS Excel 2010. Do as directed by your teacher.
2. Create the worksheet shown and then make the following changes:

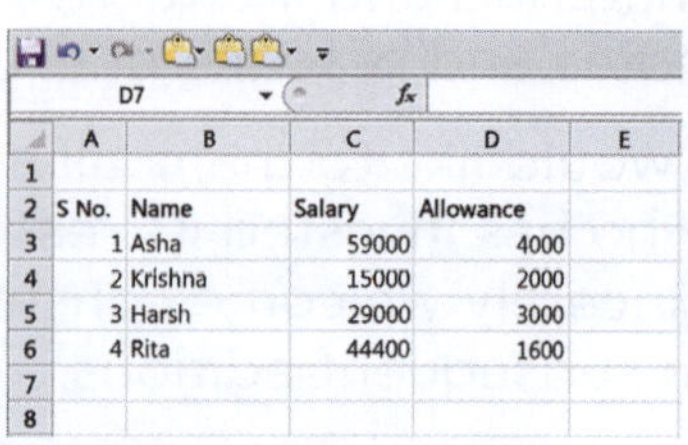

	A	B	C	D	E
1					
2	S No.	Name	Salary	Allowance	
3	1	Asha	59000	4000	
4	2	Krishna	15000	2000	
5	3	Harsh	29000	3000	
6	4	Rita	44400	1600	
7					
8					

is given to test the practical application of the concept taught

EXERCISE

A Fill in the blanks with appropriate options.

Windows Movie Maker User Interface   Video Tools Edit   Seek

1. The home page of Windows Movie Maker is known as the __________ .
2. You can start playing the movie from any place by clicking on the ________ .

Is given to reinforce understanding of the concepts covered in each chapter

FA ASSESSMENTS

ASSESSMENT 1

Chapters 1 and 2

1. Write any five advantages of using a computer. **(5)**

____

____

____

____

____

facilitates the students and teachers with additional questions for Formative Assessments

NATIONAL CYBER OLYMPIAD

1. Which of the following are used to print characters by an impact printer?
   (i) An ink pen
   (ii) Electrically charged ink
   (iii) An inked ribbon
   (iv) A print head

has questions based on NCO by Science Olympiad Foundation

SA REVISION QUESTIONS

REVISION QUESTIONS

Suggested Questions for SA

1 Colour the machines you see outside the house. **(6)**

aims at testing the students' understanding of the concepts taught and can be used as Summative Assessmen

FA WORKSHEET AND PROJECTS—3

WORKSHEET

A Choose correct option for each of the following.

1. The Flash file is saved with an extension
   (a) .fls (c) .fla
   (b) .fll (d) None of the above

2. The Rulers option is in ____________ menu.

Projects

Your school is hosting a Christmas fair. The Principal wants to upload an animated poster on the school website giving the details of the fair. Create the same using Flash 8.

reinforce the concepts by testing the students' grasping power

Collins DigiSuite is an innovative digital solution for teachers. It contains three modules delivering classroom content that can be used to effectively integrate the teaching and evaluation tools with the coursebooks.

The **e-book** includes animations, video snippets, interactive exercises, slide shows, guided tours and worksheets. The e-book reader also includes interactive teaching tools like pen tool, text highlighter, page zoom, search and bookmark.

The **Test Generator** is a question bank with a variety of questions for effective evaluation. It is an easy-to-use assessment tool for the teachers to create test papers and worksheets.

The **Teacher's Resource** consists of lesson plans, answer keys and teaching techniques for the teachers.

Contents

1 Data Storage Media

Learning Objectives

By the end of this chapter you should be able to
- learn about computer memory.
- learn about data storage devices.
- learn about binary digits.
- learn about primary, read-only and secondary memory.

Introduction

You have learnt in previous classes that we can input data into a computer using input devices. The computer then processes the input according to the instructions provided and gives the output (result) through various output devices. The computer uses its memory to store the data or the information. Apart from this, a computer can also use its memory to store the instructions.

There are various kinds of computer memory—some are permanent while others are temporary, some are inexpensive while others are expensive, some are very fast while others are relatively slow. Modern computers use a combination of different kinds of memory to provide a proper balance between storage, speed and accessibility.

You Should Know

Many modern electronic devices have an inbuilt memory which stores information and instructions. Some examples of such devices are:

(a) Smartphones and tablets
(b) Car radios
(c) Game consoles
(d) Digital cameras

COMPUTER MEMORY

The memory of a computer refers to the physical devices used to store instructions, information or data temporarily or permanently.

There are two basic kinds of computer memory—the primary memory and the secondary memory.

Before we study the characteristics and functions of these different kinds of computer memory, let us take a look at how data is represented in a computer's memory.

REPRESENTING CHARACTERS IN MEMORY

A computer uses only two digits (0 and 1) to represent all the information. Thus, any data input into the computer (for example, a user typing the letter 'A' on the keyboard or clicking the mouse) must be converted into a series of 0s and 1s for the computer to process or store it. Numbers which are represented using only the digits 0 and 1 are called **binary numbers**. For example, the decimal number 10 is represented as binary number 1010 in the computer's memory.

Computers use binary numbers in place of decimal numbers and therefore, use binary digits in place of decimal digits. The word **bit** is formed by shortening the words 'binary digit'. Decimal digits, which we usually use in our everyday lives, have 10 possible values ranging from 0 to 9; but binary digits, or bits, have only two possible values—0 and 1.

A bit or a single binary digit (which can be either 0 or 1) is the smallest unit of data a computer can handle.

Bits are usually grouped together into collections of eight. This collection of 8 bits is called a **byte**.

Thus, 1 byte = 8 bits.

You Should Know

A nibble is a collection of 4 bits.

We usually use the letter 'B' as an abbreviation for bytes.

A byte is a small unit of data. When you type one letter in a Notepad document, it represents one byte of information. Since modern computers are very efficient and deal with millions of bytes of information, we use various prefixes to form higher units of data as shown in the table below.

1 Kilobyte (KB) = 2^{10} bytes = 1024 bytes
1 Megabyte (MB) = 2^{20} bytes = 1024 KB (or 1,048,576 bytes)
1 Gigabyte (GB) = 2^{30} bytes = 1024 MB (or 1,073,741,824 bytes)
1 Terabyte (TB) = 2^{40} bytes = 1024 GB (or 1,099,511,627,776 bytes)
1 Petabyte (PB) = 2^{50} bytes = 1024 TB (or 1,125,899,906,842,624 bytes)

You Should Know

We always use the capital letter 'B' to denote a byte; a lowercase 'b' implies a 'bit'. Thus, KB stands for Kilobyte while Kb stands for Kilobit.

TYPES OF COMPUTER MEMORY

A CPU reads the data from the data storage units. Then it processes the data into information and directs the data to the output devices for storage. Modern CPUs are very powerful and fast. They can process huge amount of information in a very short time.

A CPU cannot read or write data directly from all kinds of memory. Therefore, we have to use different kinds of memory to make sure that we can read and write the data from all of them and also ensure data storage for future use.

The most basic kinds of computer memory are:

1. Primary memory or internal memory
2. Secondary memory or external memory

Let us take a look at each of these types of memory.

Primary Memory

Primary memory or internal memory (also called the main memory) is an inbuilt memory which can store data and instructions. Primary memory holds only the data and instructions on which the computer is currently working. It has limited capacity.

Primary memory is generally made up of semiconductor devices. Primary memory provides faster access, but is usually much smaller in capacity than the secondary memory units. A CPU can directly access data and instructions stored on the primary memory. Primary memory is also referred to as Random Access Memory (RAM).

Random Access Memory (RAM)

Random Access Memory (RAM) can be directly accessed by the CPU. Data can be read from the RAM and written on to it. In other words, a RAM is a read–write memory.

Fig. 1.1: Random Access Memory

A RAM can store data or instructions till the time computer is switched on. The moment the computer is switched off, the data on this memory is lost. Hence, the memory which can store data or information only temporarily is called volatile memory.

Whenever we open or load any file on the computer, it is loaded in the computer's temporary memory (RAM). Storing data on RAM makes it easier for the CPU to access information. CPU requests for the data it needs from RAM, processes it and writes back new data to RAM in a continuous cycle. The cycling of data between the CPU and RAM happens millions of times per second in modern computers. When we close a file or an application, it is usually deleted from the RAM to make room for new data. If the modified files are not saved to permanent storage device, before closing the application, they get deleted from the RAM and hence get lost.

Read-Only Memory (ROM)

ROM or read-only memory is the memory from which information can only be read and not written on to.

The processor can directly read from the ROM, but it cannot write to it or modify it in any way.

ROM is a non-volatile memory or a permanent memory. The data and instructions stored on the ROM are not erased and are stored even after the computer is switched off.

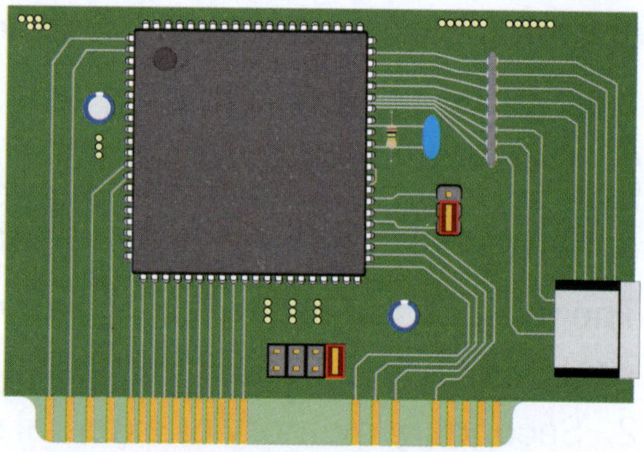

Fig. 1.2: Read-Only Memory

Various writeable and editable ROMs are available nowadays. Some examples of ROMs are as follows:

(a) PROM—Programmable Read-Only Memory

(b) EPROM—Erasable Programmable Read-Only Memory

(c) EEPROM—Electrically Erasable Programmable Read-Only Memory

You Should Know

BIOS is the Basic Input Output System and is also known as ROM BIOS. It is the first software run by a PC when powered on.

Secondary Memory

Primary memory is very fast and can be directly accessed by the processor. But it is volatile and it has limited capacity. It cannot be used to store large amount of data permanently.

So, we use secondary memory or auxiliary memory units to store large amount of data permanently. It can retain the information stored on it even after the computer has been switched off.

The secondary storage devices usually have a much larger storage capacity than the primary storage units. Secondary memory cannot be directly accessed by the CPU. The data to be used is first moved to the primary memory from the secondary memory. Then the CPU can access that information. The primary memory units are made from semiconductors while the secondary storage devices are mostly magnetic or optical in nature.

The table below mentions the points of difference between the primary memory and the secondary memory.

Primary Memory	Secondary Memory
The primary memory is made up of semiconductor devices.	The secondary memory devices are usually magnetic or optical.
The primary memory is always volatile.	The secondary memory is always non-volatile.
The primary memory is used to store instructions and data that are presently being used by the CPU. The data stored on primary memory is lost once the computer is switched off.	The secondary memory is used to store large amount of information even after the computer is switched off.
The CPU can directly access the primary memory.	The CPU cannot directly access the secondary memory.
Primary memory is usually referred to as internal memory.	Secondary memory is usually referred to as external memory.
Most modern personal computers have RAM between 512 MB and 8 GB.	Secondary memory can be as large as a disk with a capacity of 4 TB.

Hard disks are the most commonly used secondary storage units. Other commonly used secondary memory units are floppy disks, CDs, DVDs, Blu-ray discs and flash drives or pen drives. Let us take a look at some common secondary storage devices.

Hard Disk

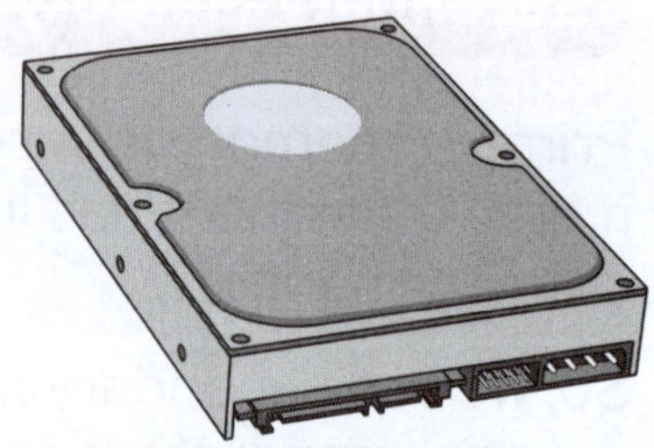

Fig. 1.3: Hard Disk

A hard disk is the most commonly used form of secondary memory. It was invented by IBM (International Business Machines) in 1956. Modern hard disks can be as large as 4 TB or 8 TB. Hard disk acts as a storehouse of information. A hard disk is a magnetic storage device and it uses magnetic spots to represent the bits (presence of a magnetic spot represents the number 1 and its absence denotes the number 0). There are two types of hard disks—internal hard disk (placed inside the cabinet) and external hard disk (connected to the computer through cables).

You Should Know

A floppy disk (1.44 MB storage capacity) is a comparatively smaller secondary storage device which could be used to store or transfer data. It is a magnetic storage device, rarely used nowadays as it has small storage capacity. The figure shows a 3.5-inch floppy disk.

Floppy Disk

CD

Fig. 1.4: CD-ROM

A CD-ROM (Compact Disc Read-Only Memory), or simply a CD, is an optical storage media which can be used to store data. A CD can store up to 900 MB of data and can be read using a CD-ROM drive. There are generally two types of CD-ROMs:

1. CD-R (Compact Disc–Recordable): It refers to a CD from which we can just read the data. The data written onto this CD cannot be erased off.
2. CD-RW (Compact Disc–Rewritable): It refers to a CD from which we can read and modify the data. We can also add new data to the existing data. It is also referred to as erasable CD.

DVD

A DVD (Digital Versatile Disc) is also an optical storage media, like the CD, which can be used to store data. However, a DVD is much larger in capacity than a CD. It can store data up to 4.7 GB.

Fig. 1.5: DVD

Blu-ray Disc

A Blu-ray disc is an optical secondary storage media and has a much larger storage capacity than a CD or a DVD.

Typically, a single Blu-ray disc can accommodate up to 25 GB data.

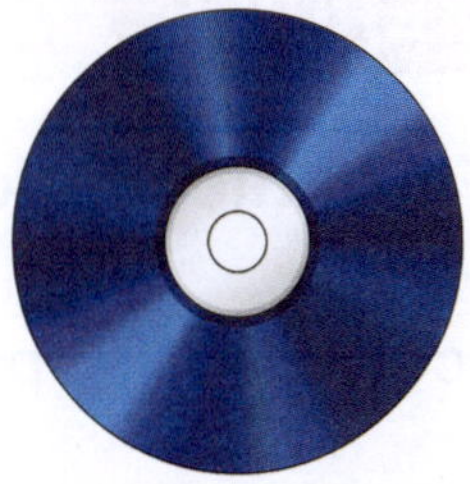

Fig. 1.6: Blu-ray disc

Pen Drive

A pen drive or a flash drive is another secondary storage device.

A pen drive is very small in size and can be carried easily. So, it is a good medium to transfer information from one computer to another.

Fig. 1.7: Pen drive

A pen drive is connected to the computer using any of the USB ports in the cabinet.

Quick Recap

1. The memory of a computer refers to the physical devices used to store instructions, information or data temporarily or permanently.
2. A computer uses only two digits (0 and 1) to represent all the information. A bit or a single binary digit (which can be either 0 or 1) is the smallest unit of data that a computer can handle. Bits are usually grouped together into collections of eight which are called bytes.
3. There are two basic kinds of computer memory—the primary memory and the secondary memory.
4. Primary memory or internal memory is also called the main memory. It is an inbuilt memory which can store data or instructions. Primary memory holds only the data and instructions on which the computer is currently working. It has a limited capacity.
5. Primary memory is also referred to as Random Access Memory (RAM).
6. Read-Only Memory (ROM) is the memory from which information can only be read and not written on to. There are various types of writeable and editable ROMs.
7. Secondary memory or auxiliary memory units are used to store large amount of data permanently. They can retain the information stored on them even after the computer is switched off.
8. Some common types of secondary storage units are floppy disks, CDs, DVDs, Blu-ray discs and pen drives or flash drives.

EXERCISE

A **Fill in the blanks with appropriate words.**

secondary   primary   digital versatile disc   optical   instructions

1. A computer uses storage devices to store data and ______________.
2. DVD stands for ______________________________.
3. The ______________ memory can be directly accessed by the CPU.
4. The ______________ memory is always non-volatile.
5. A CD is an ______________ storage device.

B **Complete the table given below:**

1. 1 KB = __________ bytes
2. 1 __________ = 2^{30} bytes
3. 1 PB = __________ bytes
4. 1 __________ = 2^{20} bytes

Which is the highest unit of measurement?

C **State whether the following statements are true (T) or false (F).**

1. 'B' is used to denote a bit. ☐
2. Bits are grouped together into collections of tens. ☐
3. A CPU can directly access data stored on the primary memory. ☐
4. Blue-ray disc can accomodate up to 25 GB of data. ☐

D **Write about each of the following.**

1. Blu-ray disc
2. Pen drive
3. Hard disk
4. Auxiliary memory
5. Main memory

E Answer the following questions.

1. What is a computer memory?
2. What is a bit? How is it related to a byte?
3. What is the difference between RAM and ROM?
4. Write any three differences between primary memory and secondary memory?
5. Write the names of any three secondary storage devices.

Lab Activity

FA

Visit your school computer lab. Form groups of six students in each group. Observe a cabinet in the lab and try to locate the following:

CD/DVD Drive   USB port   Floppy drive

Now, with the permission of your teacher, try to access files from any CD, DVD and, if possible, a floppy disk. Also, request your teacher to provide you with a CD-R and a CD-RW. Try to use them and list their differences in your notebook.

Research Project

FA

1. Make a chart to pictorially represent the classification of computer memory. Use the following points for the comparison:
   (a) capacity
   (b) speed
   (c) can be accessed directly by the CPU or not
   (d) types and examples of each kind of memory
2. Use the Internet to find more about BIOS. Discuss in class about the various uses of BIOS and the tasks it helps us to perform.

Teacher's Note

Teachers should explain the flow of data from the memory to the CPU. Additionally, proper handling of CDs and DVDs should be demonstrated.

The teacher can also show how to attach a pen drive to a computer, how to load data on it and how to safely remove it.

2 Flowcharting

Learning Objectives

By the end of this chapter you should be able to
- learn about algorithms.
- learn about flowcharts.
- learn about the methods of flowcharting.

Introduction

To do any task, we need to follow a sequence of steps. This sequence of steps helps us in completing the task correctly. For example, to make tea we need to follow the steps given below:

1. Pour water in the kettle.
2. Add tea leaves.
3. Bring the mixture to a boil.
4. Sieve and pour in a cup.
5. If you want, add warm milk.
6. Add sugar according to your taste.
7. Serve.

For cooking, we use a recipe which is a set of step-by-step instructions to be followed in order to prepare a particular dish. While giving road directions, we give step-by-step instructions (go straight, turn left when you reach the crossing, etc). Many modern gadgets and appliances come with manuals which contain step-by-step instructions on how to operate the gadget to perform a specific task.

These step-by-step instructions to perform a particular task are called algorithms.

In other words, algorithm is a step-by-step approach to solve a problem. We write step-by-step instructions in natural language to develop a solution for a problem. These set of instructions when coded in any programming language are known as programs.

The computer programs help us to communicate with the computer. The algorithms are generally written in natural language (English) or pseudocodes.

You Should Know

Pseudocode refers to the combination of any natural language and structural components of any programming language.

Practice Time 1

Can you write the step-by-step instructions to do the following on a computer?

(a) Reading an online newspaper
(b) Starting a computer running on Windows 7 operating system
(c) Drawing a square with each side 100 units in MSWLogo

ALGORITHMS

In computing, an algorithm is a series of sequential procedures (step-by-step instructions) for performing calculations or processing data. Algorithms are independent of computer programming languages—they can be converted into any programming language.

Algorithms must be clear, precise and unambiguous. If the algorithm is vague or unclear, the results derived using the algorithm will also be inaccurate. Thus, multiple sets of instructions or algorithms when coded in any programming language form a computer program.

Word Web

Unambiguous: clear; well defined

Let us study the following algorithms.

Calculate and print the sum of two numbers.

1. Start.
2. Read the first number. Store it as X. (X)
3. Read the second number. Store it as Y. (Y)

4. Add the two numbers. Store it as Sum. (Sum = X+Y)
5. Print Sum.
6. Stop.

Calculate and print the average of two numbers.

1. Start.
2. Read the first number. Store it as X. (X)
3. Read the second number. Store it as Y. (Y)
4. Add the two numbers. Store it as Sum. (Sum = X+Y)
5. Divide Sum by 2 to get the average. Store it as Avg. (Avg = Sum/2)
6. Print Avg.
7. Stop.

Compare two numbers to find out which one is smaller and print the result.

1. Start.
2. Read the first number. Store it as X.
3. Read the second number. Store it as Y.
4. Check if X=Y or not. If X=Y, go to step 5, else go to step 6.
5. Print "The numbers are equal". Go to step 9.
6. Check if X<Y go to step 7, else go to step 8.
7. Print "X is smaller". Go to step 9.
8. Print "Y is smaller".
9. Stop.

Check if a given number is even or odd.

1. Read the number. Store it as X.
2. Divide X by 2 and find the remainder. Store the remainder as R.
3. If R=0, print "The number is even". Go to step 5.
4. If R=1, print "The number is odd".
5. Stop.

Practice Time 2

Write the algorithms for the following.

(a) Find and print the difference of two numbers A and B, where A is greater than B.
(b) Find and print the product of two numbers A and B.
(c) Find if a number is divisible by 3.

FLOWCHARTS

We have already seen that an algorithm gives us a set of step-by-step instructions to perform a task.

A flowchart is a graphical or symbolic representation of the sequential instructions necessary to perform a task. It is a very useful concept to learn programming. It guides us to write clear and simple programs. We can also break difficult programs into multiple simpler and smaller programs, and then merge them to find a solution.

A typical flowchart to calculate the sum of two numbers looks like the one given below:

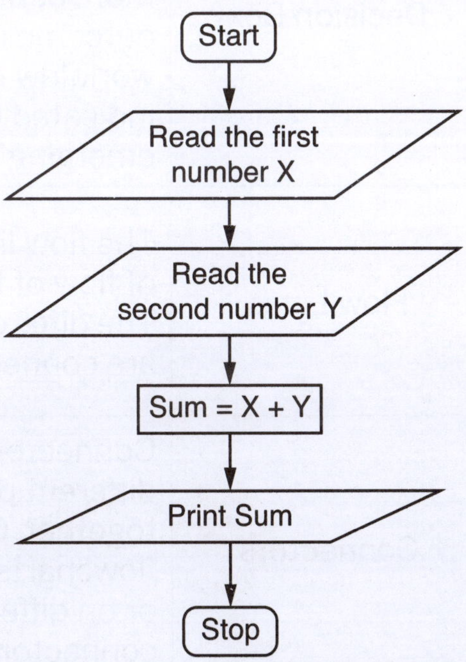

Fig. 2.1: Flowchart to add two numbers

This is a flowchart to describe the steps involved in calculating and printing the sum of two numbers. As you can see from the flowchart, symbols are linked together with arrows showing the direction of the flow of the process. The flowchart has different symbols, each of which is used for specific purpose.

Let us take a look at some of the different types of flowchart symbols.

Symbol	Name of the Box	Description
	Start/Stop Box	It is used to mark the beginning and end of a flowchart. A flowchart can have only one start box and only one stop box.
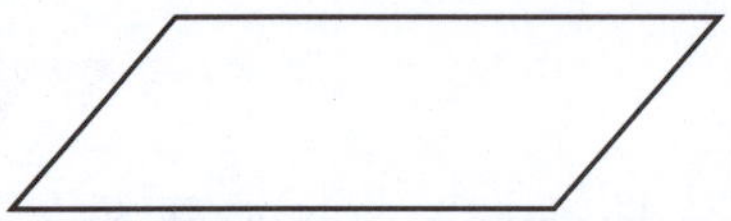	Input/Output Box	It is used for taking inputs or giving outputs.
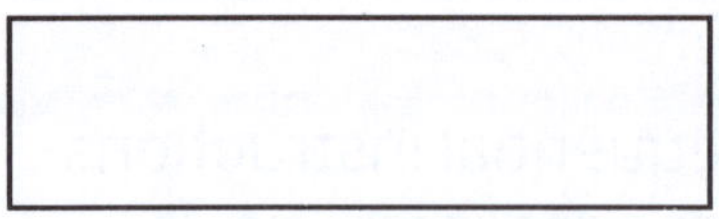	Process Box	This is used to mark the processing or calculation instructions, like adding or subtracting numbers.
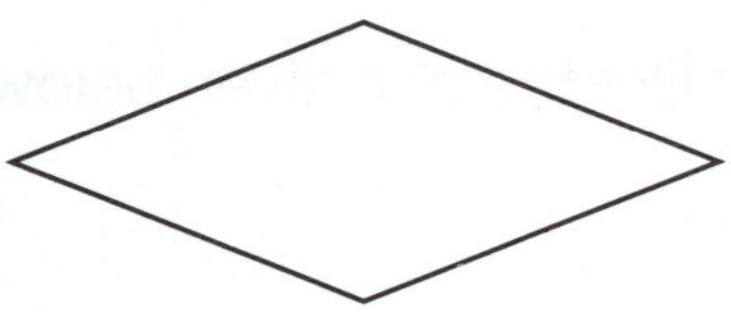	Decision Box	The decision box is used when the process asks a question and has to choose between two or more actions depending upon the outcome of a calculation. Often the workflow is split in a decision box, indicated by two or more flow lines emerging from the decision box.
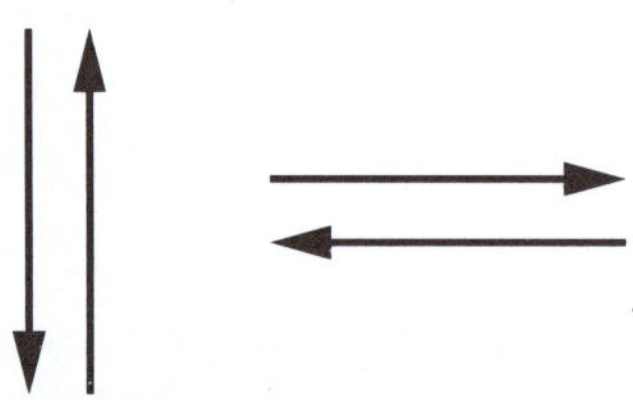	Flow Lines	The flow lines indicate the direction of flow of the instructions/process. The different boxes in the flowchart are connected with flow lines.
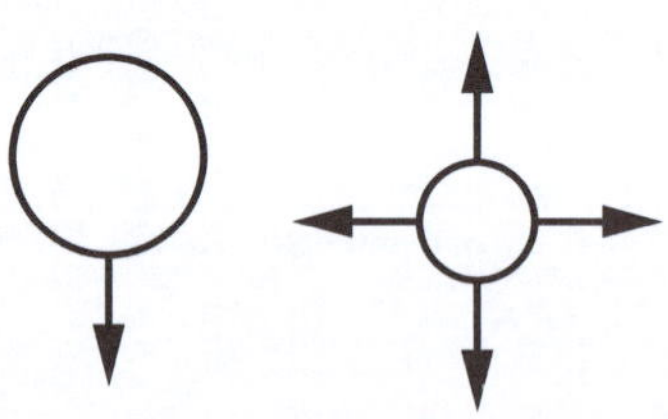	Connectors	Connectors are used to connect different parts of flowcharts together. Connectors may connect flowcharts on the same page or on different pages (off-page connectors).

You Should Know

Usually, the direction of the flow of process in a flowchart is either from left to right or from top to bottom.

The following flowcharts demonstrate the use of decision boxes and other flowcharting symbols.

A flowchart to compare two numbers and identify the smaller one

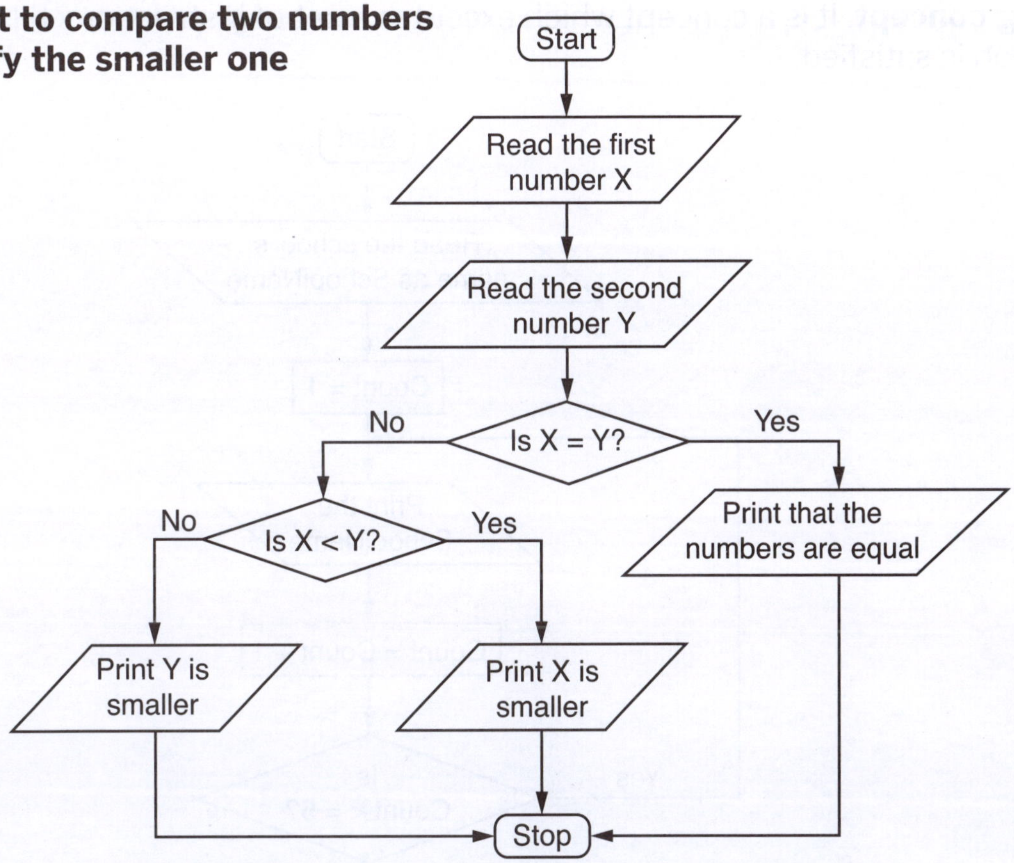

Fig. 2.2: Flowchart to find the smaller of two numbers

A flowchart to find if a number is even or odd

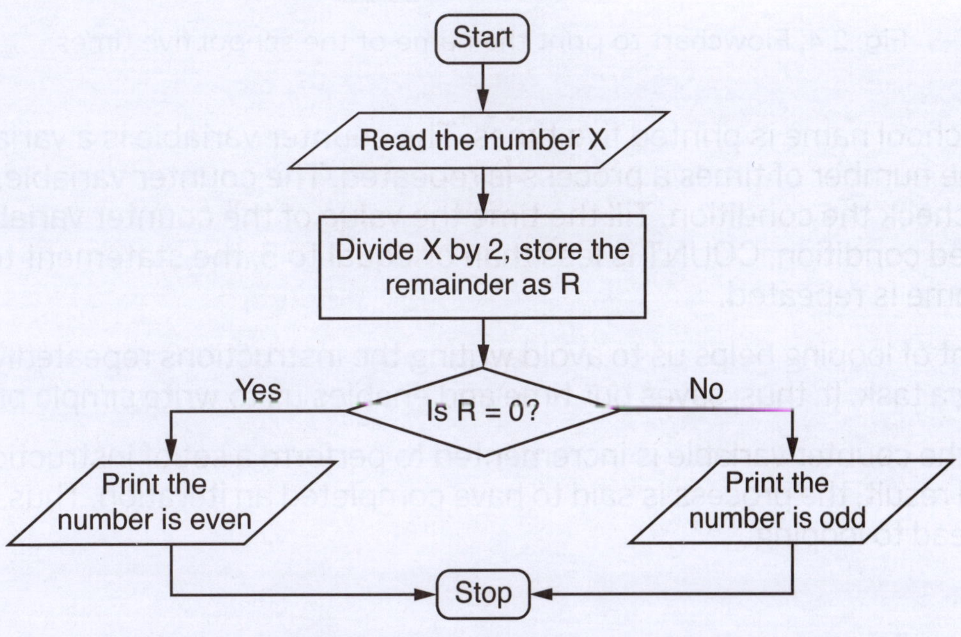

Fig. 2.3: Flowchart to find if a number is even or odd

A flowchart to print the name of your school five times

This flowchart will help you do the same task repeatedly. It is based on the **looping concept**. It is a concept which executes a set of instructions till the condition is satisfied.

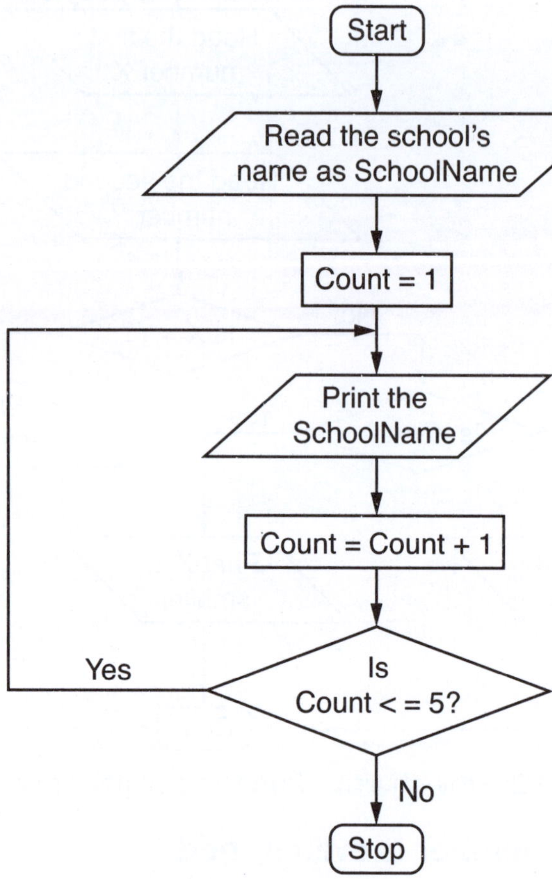

Fig. 2.4: Flowchart to print the name of the school five times

Here, the school name is printed five times. The counter variable is a variable used to count the number of times a process is repeated. The counter variable, COUNT is used to check the condition. Till the time the value of the counter variable meets the specified condition, COUNT is less than or equal to 5, the statement to print the school's name is repeated.

The concept of looping helps us to avoid writing the instructions repeatedly for completing a task. It, thus, saves our time and enables us to write simple programs.

Each time the counter variable is incremented to perform a set of instructions to get the desired result, the process is said to have completed an iteration. Thus, multiple iterations lead to looping.

Quick Recap

1. In computing, an algorithm is a series of sequential procedures for performing calculations or processing data. They are independent of any computer programming languages.
2. Algorithms must be clear, precise and unambiguous.
3. A flowchart is a graphical or symbolic representation of the sequential instructions necessary to perform a task. It uses different kinds of symbols and flow lines to formulate the workflow.
4. The start/stop box is used to mark the beginning/end of a flowchart. A flowchart can have only one start box and only one stop box.
5. The input/output box is used for taking inputs or giving outputs.
6. The process box is used to mark the processing or calculating instructions, like adding or subtracting numbers.
7. The decision box is used when the process asks a question and has to choose between two or more actions depending upon the answer. Often the workflow is split in a decision box, indicated by two or more flow lines emerging from the decision box.
8. The flow lines indicate the direction of the flow of the instructions/ process. The different boxes in the flowchart are connected with flow lines. Usually, the direction of workflow is either from left to right or from top to bottom.
9. Connectors are used to connect different parts of flowcharts together. Connectors may connect flowcharts on the same page or on different pages (off-page connectors).
10. Looping concept is a concept which executes a set of instructions till the condition is satisfied.
11. Iterations refer to the number of times a particular loop is executed.

EXERCISE

A Fill in the blanks using the words given below.

decision   flow lines   input/output   process   start/stop

1. The ____________ box is used to mark the beginning or end of a flowchart.
2. The ____________ box is used for taking inputs or giving outputs.
3. The ____________ box is used to mark the processing or calculation instructions, like adding or subtracting numbers.

4. The ______________ box is used when the process asks a question and has to choose between two or more actions depending on the answer.
5. The ______________ indicate the direction of the flow of the instructions/process.

B Match the following.

	Symbol	Name of the Box
(a)	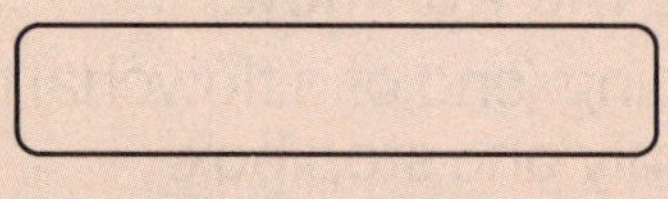	(i) Connectors
(b)	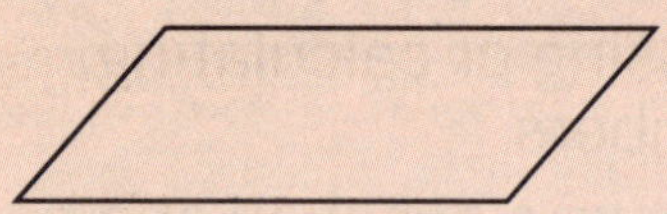	(ii) Process Box
(c)	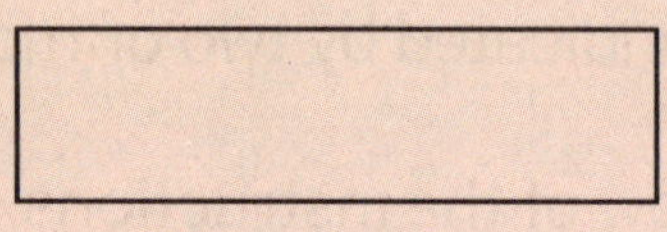	(iii) Decision Box
(d)	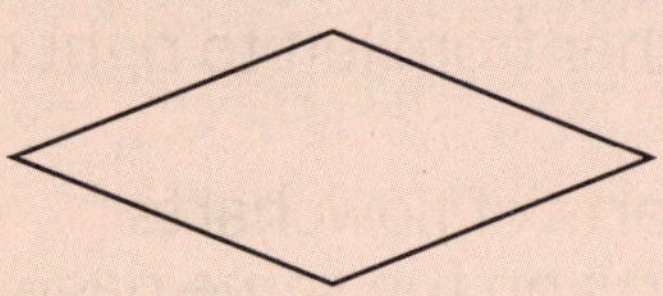	(iv) Flow Lines
(e)	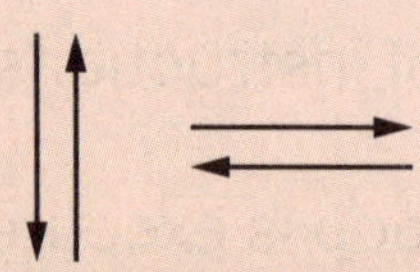	(v) Input/Output Box
(f)	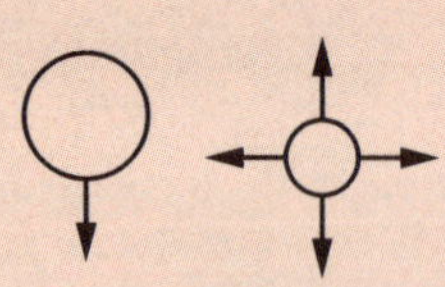	(vi) Start/Stop box

C Write the algorithms and draw flowcharts for the following.

1. Calculate and print the sum of three numbers.
2. Calculate and print the average of three numbers.
3. Find out the bigger number among the two given numbers.

D Answer the following questions.

1. What are algorithms? In what languages can the algorithms be written?
2. What are flowcharts? Name the different symbols used in a flowchart.
3. What are the two directions of workflow?
4. What are connectors?
5. Explain the looping concept.

Lab Activity

FA

Write the algorithms and then draw the following flowcharts in MS Word 2010.

(a) A flowchart showing how to make milkshake.
(b) A flowchart showing how to save a file in MS Word.
(c) A flowchart showing how to print the table of 2.

Research Project

FA

You already know how to write the algorithm for comparing two numbers and pointing out which number is smaller. Use this knowledge to write an algorithm to find the smallest number among the three given numbers.

Now, draw a flowchart for this algorithm. How many decision boxes does this flowchart have?

Research on the Internet how mathematics and computer science are related. Discuss with your teacher how the algorithms helped to prepare the software application called calculator.

Teacher's Note

Teachers should explain how algorithms are useful, especially how they form the basis for programming concepts.

The teachers should also emphasize the use of proper symbols while flowcharting and explain the concept of workflow and decision boxes.

The teachers should encourage students to practice drawing the flowcharts for the tasks listed at the end of this book. This will help the students to grasp the logic-building concept and prepare a base for programming.

3 Procedures in MSWLogo

Learning Objectives

By the end of this chapter you should be able to
- know about procedures in MSWLogo.
- know how to write and save a new procedure.
- know how to edit or delete a procedure.

Introduction

You must have come across the word *procedure*—it is a way of acting or progressing in a course of action. We follow standard procedures for many everyday tasks like switching on the computer, making an online ticket reservation, etc.

In MSWLogo, a set of commands can be stored as a **MSWLogo procedure** with a particular name. Generally, we save the commands that are repeatedly used as MSWLogo procedure. These procedures can be saved and used whenever required.

A procedure in MSWLogo can have any name formed using alphanumeric characters and special symbols with the following restrictions:

1. The name of the procedure cannot be the same as a MSWLogo command. For example, you cannot name a procedure FORWARD or FD.
2. The name cannot contain spaces or arithmetic operators (+, -, *, /).
3. The first letter of the name must be an alphabet.

Thus, TRIANGLE, SQUARE100, HOUSE911 are valid MSWLogo procedure names, while BACKWARD, 1CLASS, X*Y, SUBTRACT4-3 are not.

Practice Time 1

Say which of the following are not valid MSWLogo procedures and why.

(a) FORWARD10
(b) 1010BINARY
(c) REPEAT
(d) SQUARE
(e) A+B
(f) PETER1
(g) HOME
(h) 3*9
(i) SMART
(j) BIG SQUARE
(k) LT
(l) 9MACHINE

PROCEDURES

Now that we know how to name a procedure, let us take a look at how it helps us with MSWLogo programming.

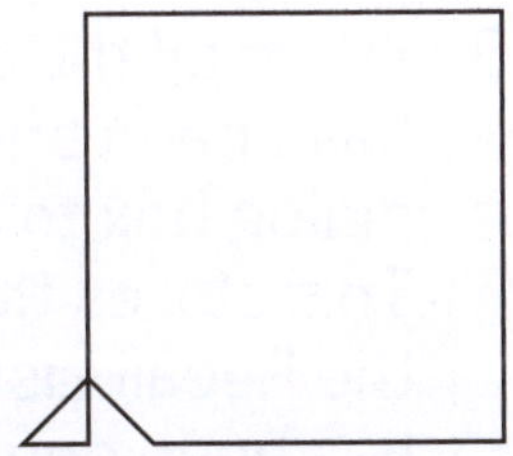

In MSWLogo, some commands or group of commands are often repeated as a set.

For example, when we enter the command REPEAT 4 [FD 100 RT 90] in the input box of the commander window, we get the output in the main (or output) screen as shown in adjacent figure.

Now, MSWLogo allows us to define a procedure to store the commands needed to draw a square. Let us name this procedure as SQUARE.

Once the commands are saved as the procedure, instead of writing REPEAT 4 [FD 100 RT 90] every time we want to draw a square, we can just type the name SQUARE to recall the procedure to draw the square.

A procedure in MSWLogo always has the following three parts:

(a) **The first line or the title line**: This line has the word *To* followed by the name of the procedure. For example, To SQUARE, To CLASS1.
(b) **The body**: This part contains the sequential list of commands that the procedure will execute.
(c) **The end line**: This line contains the word *End* to indicate the end of the procedure.

Thus, a typical procedure would look like the one as follows:

```
To SQUARE
REPEAT 4 [FD 100 RT 90]
End
```

HOW TO DEFINE A PROCEDURE

We can define a procedure in MSWLogo in two different ways. Let us take a look at both the ways.

Using the Input Box

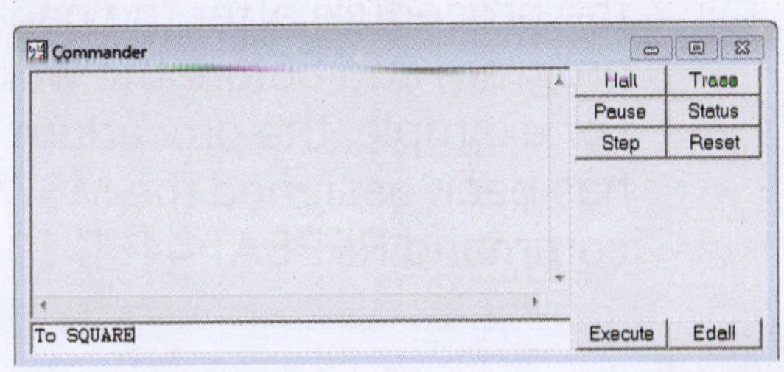

To define a procedure in MSWLogo using the input box in the commander window, follow these steps:

1. In the input box, write *To* followed by the name of the procedure (for example, To SQUARE) and press the Enter key.

2. This opens the **To Mode** dialog box with the option to provide MSWLogo primitives one after another by pressing the Enter key after each command or set of commands.

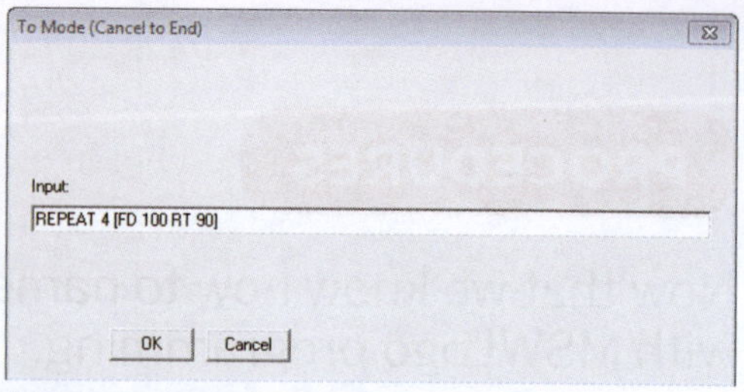

3. When all the commands for the procedure have been entered, type *End* in the **To Mode** dialog box to end defining the procedure. This closes the **To Mode** dialog box and the Recall List box shows that a procedure has been defined with the given name (for example, SQUARE defined).

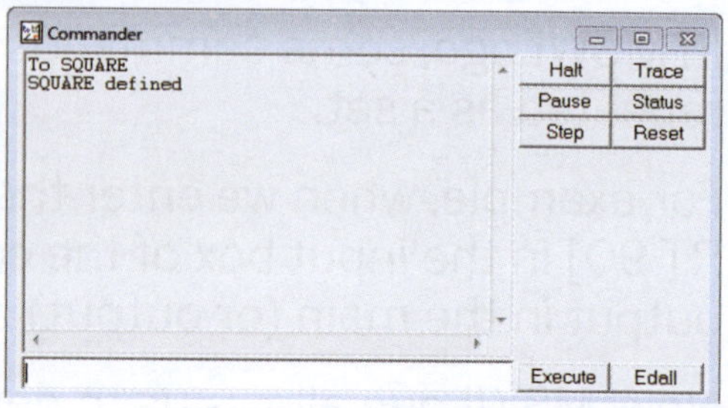

4. To run the procedure, simply type the name of the procedure in the input box and press Enter. For example, if we write SQUARE in the input box and press Enter we will get the output as shown here. Note that this figure, which shows the output for using the procedure SQUARE is exactly the same as the previous one, which was the output obtained by using the set of commands REPEAT 4 [FD 100 RT 90].

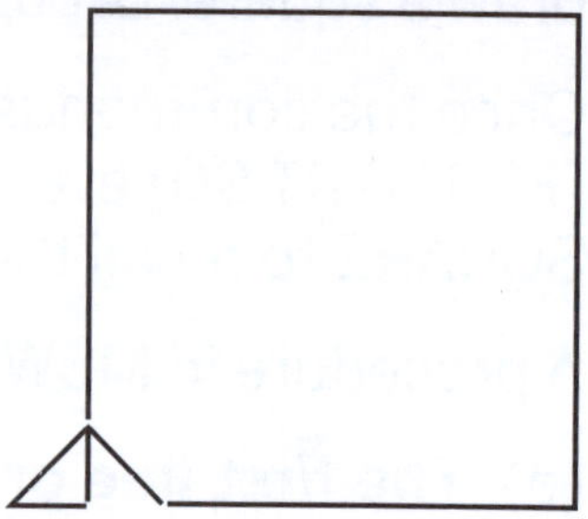

Using the Edit command from the File Menu

To define a procedure in MSWLogo using the File menu in the MSWLogo screen, follow these steps:

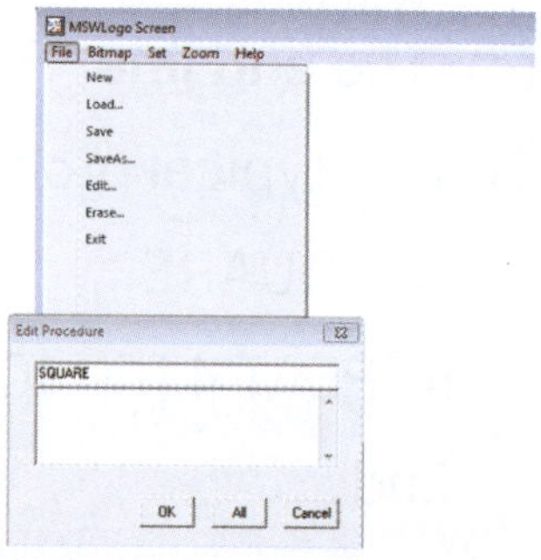

1. On the Main window, click on **File** to open the File menu.
2. Click on **Edit** in the File menu. This opens the **Edit Procedure** dialog box.
3. Type the name of the procedure in the top box and press Enter.
4. This opens the **Editor** window with the first and the end line of the procedure already written. Write the commands you want to enter for the procedure after the name of the program and before the word *End*. For example, the procedure SQUARE has been assigned the MSWLogo command REPEAT 4 [FD 100 RT 90].

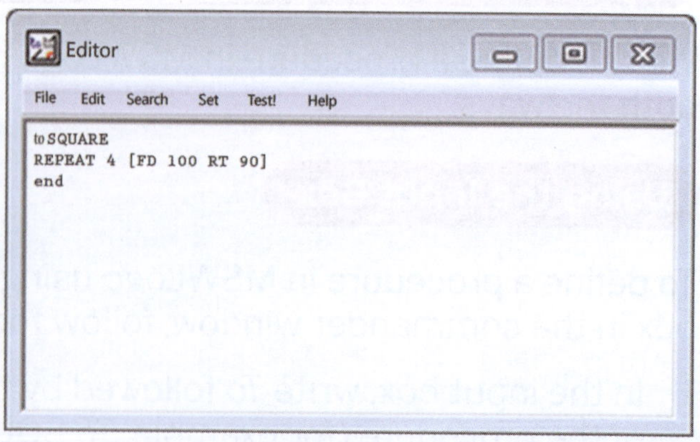

5. Click on **File** in the Editor window to open the respective File menu.
6. Click on **Save and Exit** to define the procedure with the given name.
7. To run the procedure, simply type the name of the procedure in the input box and press Enter. Note that, if we run the procedure SQUARE defined in this manner, the output is same as the figure drawn using the procedure written in the input box.

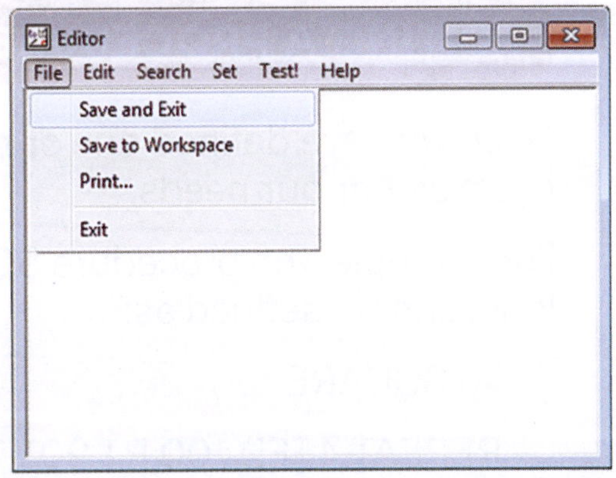

USING PROCEDURES TO FORM OTHER COMMANDS OR PROCEDURES

Once a procedure has been defined, we can use that procedure inside another MSWLogo command or to define another procedure.

Consider the following example.

Let us define the procedure TRIANGLE as:

```
To TRIANGLE
REPEAT 3 [FD 100 RT 120]
End
```

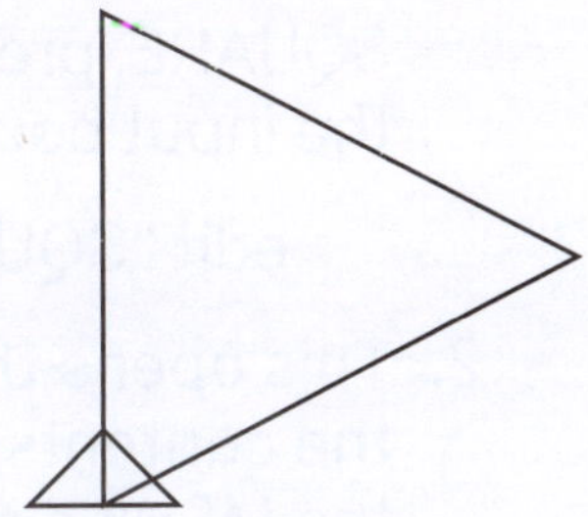

After we have defined this procedure using any of the two methods described above, writing TRIANGLE in the input box and pressing Enter will generate the output as shown in the above figure.

Now we can use this procedure with another MSWLogo command like REPEAT.

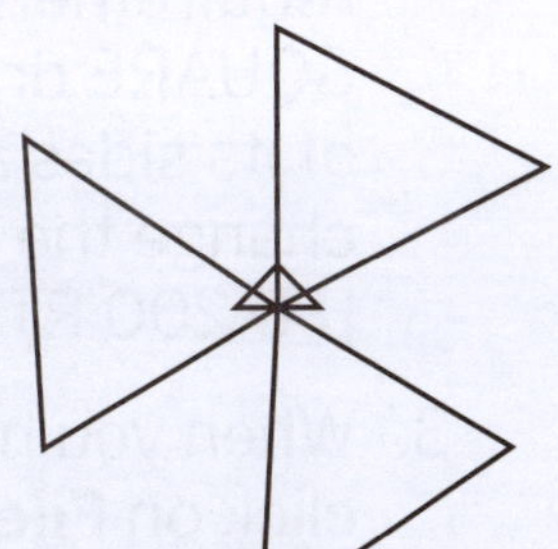

The command REPEAT 3 [TRIANGLE RT 120] will generate the output as shown in the adjacent figure.

We can even define another procedure which uses the procedure TRIANGLE. For example, we can define a procedure HEXAGON using the procedure TRIANGLE:

```
To HEXAGON
REPEAT 6 [TRIANGLE RT 60]
End
```

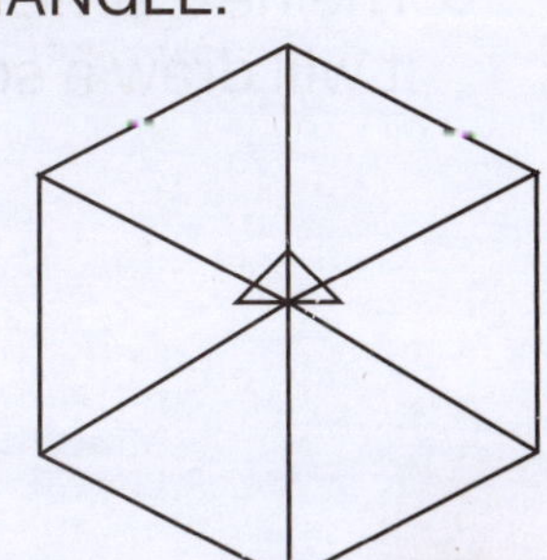

After the procedure has been defined, typing HEXAGON in the input box and pressing Enter will generate the output as shown in the figure.

EDITING A PROCEDURE

Once we have defined one or more procedures in MSWLogo, we can modify or edit them as per our needs.

For example, the procedure SQUARE, which draws a square with each side 100 units long, can be defined as:

To SQUARE

REPEAT 4 [FD 100 RT 90]

End

If we want to edit the procedure, we have to follow these steps:

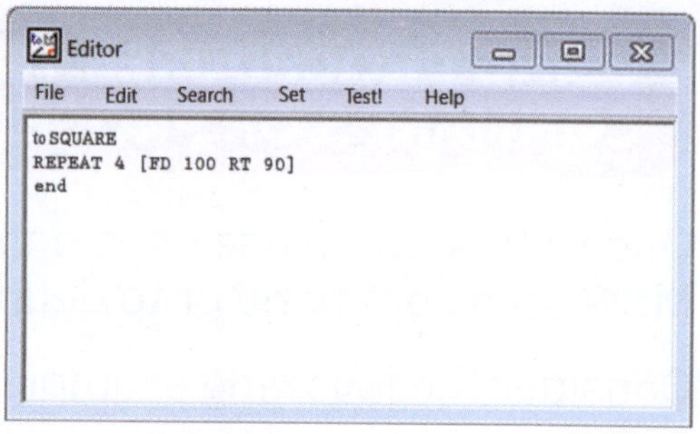

1. In the input box, write *Edit "procedure name* (there is a space after Edit and a double quote mark before the name of the procedure) and press Enter. For example, to edit the procedure SQUARE, press the Enter key after writing in the input box:

   edit "SQUARE

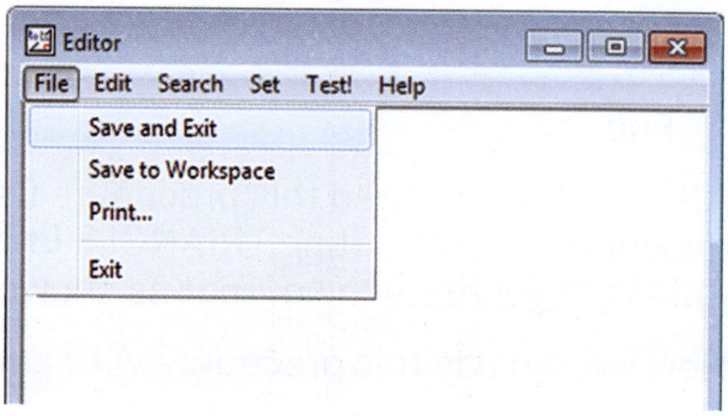

2. This opens the **Editor** window showing the contents of the procedure. Edit the MSWLogo primitives as per your requirement. To make the procedure SQUARE draw a square with each of its sides as 200 units, we have to change the primitive to REPEAT 4 [FD 200 RT 90].
3. When you have made all the changes, click on **File** in the Editor window to open the respective File menu. Click on **Save and Exit** to save the changed procedure.

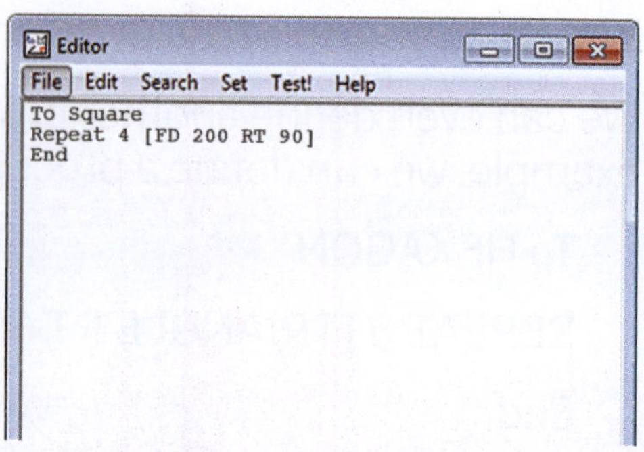

The next time you run the procedure SQUARE, it will draw a square with each side 200 units long.

You Should Know

We can see all the procedures that are currently defined by clicking on the **Edall** button in the Commander window.

Pressing the **Edall** button opens the **Editor** window which lists all the procedures defined so far.

We can edit any of the procedures using this method also.

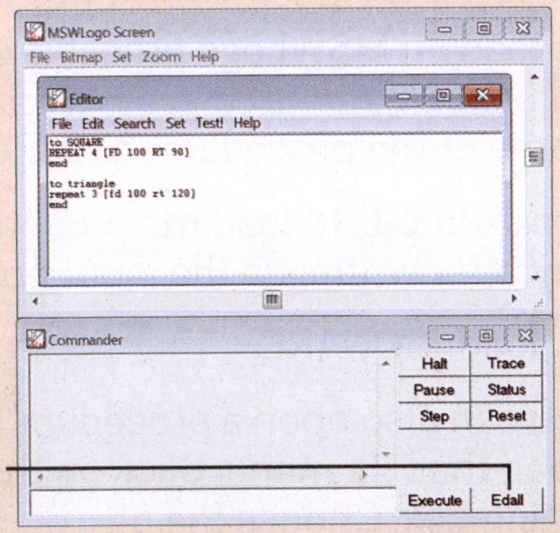

Edall button

SAVING A PROCEDURE

Just defining a procedure does not save it. The procedure remains in the volatile memory of the computer and will be lost when you exit the program. Saving the procedure moves it to the secondary storage units which store the procedure permanently.

To save an MSWLogo procedure using a primitive in the input box, write *Save "procedure name* (there is a space after Save and a double quote mark before the name of the procedure) and press Enter.

For example, to save the procedure SQUARE, press the Enter key after writing in the input box:

save "SQUARE

You can also save a procedure by clicking on **File** in the output window to open the **File** menu and clicking on the **Save** option.

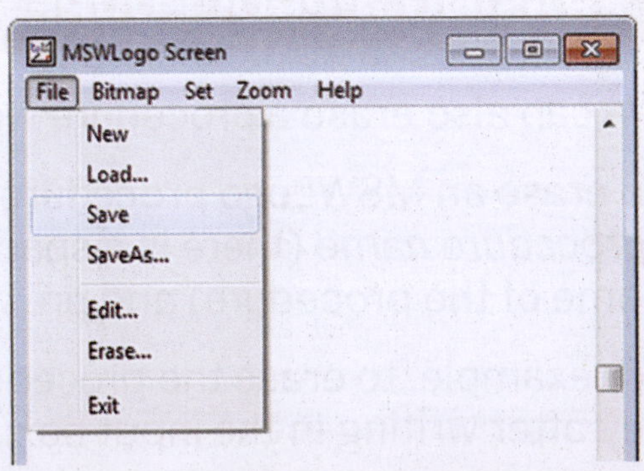

Practice Time 2

Define a procedure which will draw a square with each side as 20 units. Name this procedure SMALLSQUARE and save it. Write the steps you have followed.

Could you have named the procedure SMALL SQUARE? If not, why?

LOADING A PROCEDURE

To load an MSWLogo procedure using a primitive in the input box, write *Load "procedure name* (there is a space after Load and a double quote mark before the name of the procedure) and press Enter.

For example, to load the procedure SQUARE we saved previously, press the Enter key after writing in the input box:

load "SQUARE

You can also open a procedure by clicking on **File** in the output window. This will open the **File** menu. Click on the **Load** option. This will further open the **Open** dialog box. Choose the file you want to open and click on the **Open** button.

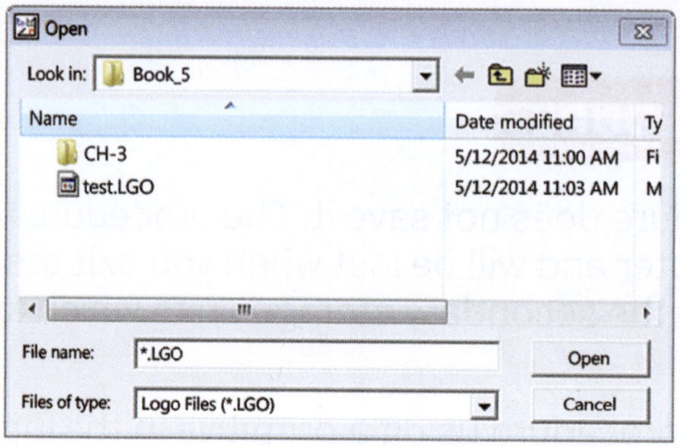

ERASING A PROCEDURE

We can also erase a procedure we have already saved in MSWLogo.

To erase an MSWLogo procedure using a primitive in the input box, write *Erase "procedure name* (there is a space after Erase and a double quote mark before the name of the procedure) and press Enter.

For example, to erase the procedure SQUARE we saved previously, press the Enter key after writing in the input box:

erase "SQUARE

This will erase the procedure SQUARE. If you try to run the procedure SQUARE, you will see an error message in the recall list box saying 'I don't know how to SQUARE'.

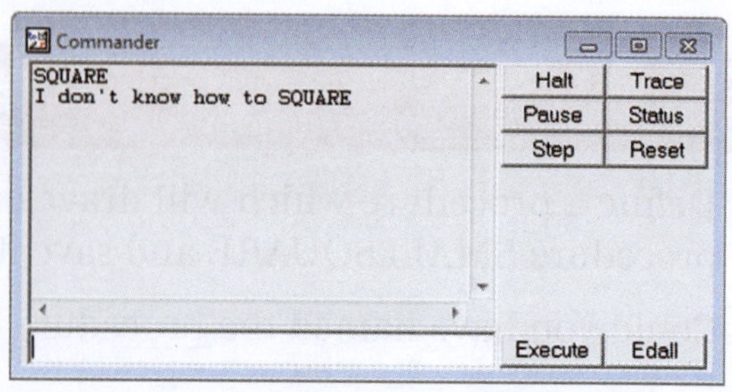

Quick Recap

1. MSWLogo procedures are defined as sequential sets of MSWLogo commands.
2. A procedure in MSWLogo can have any name using alphanumeric characters and special symbols with the following restrictions:
   (a) The name of the procedure cannot be the same as a MSWLogo command.
   (b) The name cannot contain spaces or arithmetic operators.
   (c) The first letter of the name must be an alphabet.
3. A procedure in MSWLogo always has the following three parts:
   (a) The first line or the title line: This line has the word To followed by the name of the procedure. For example, *To* SQUARE or To CLASS1.
   (b) The body: This part contains the sequential list of the commands that the procedure will execute.
   (c) The end line: This line contains the word *End* to indicate the end of the procedure.
4. Procedures can be used with other procedures or MSWLogo commands.
5. Procedures can be defined, edited, saved, loaded and erased according to the requirement.
6. The Edall button opens an Editor window which lists all the procedures defined earlier.

EXERCISE

A Fill in the blanks using the words given below.

End　　Edall　　arithmetic operator　　edit "TIGER　　save "TIGER

1. The name of an MSWLogo procedure cannot have an ____________.
2. The word ____________ forms the end line of an MSWLogo procedure.
3. The ____________ button opens an Editor window which lists all the procedures defined earlier. We can edit any of the procedures in this editor window.
4. To save an MSWLogo procedure called TIGER, you have to type ____________ in the input box and press the Enter key.
5. To edit an MSWLogo procedure called TIGER, you have to type ____________ in the input box and press the Enter key.

B State whether the following statements are true (T) or false (F).

1. 99 CIRCLES is a valid MSWLogo procedure name.
2. A procedure in MSWLogo always has three parts.
3. A procedure cannot be used inside another procedure.
4. Saving the procedure moves it to the volatile memory of the computer.
5. Procedure can be edited in the editor window.

C Write the steps involved in the following.

1. Create a procedure called SCHOOL in MSWLogo which outputs the name of your school in the main screen.
2. Save a procedure in MSWLogo.
3. Edit an existing procedure called HEXAGON.
4. Erase a procedure called CIRCLE.

FA

Lab Activity

1. Define a procedure called SQUARE to draw a square with each of its sides as 20 units. Now, use this procedure to draw the following figure:

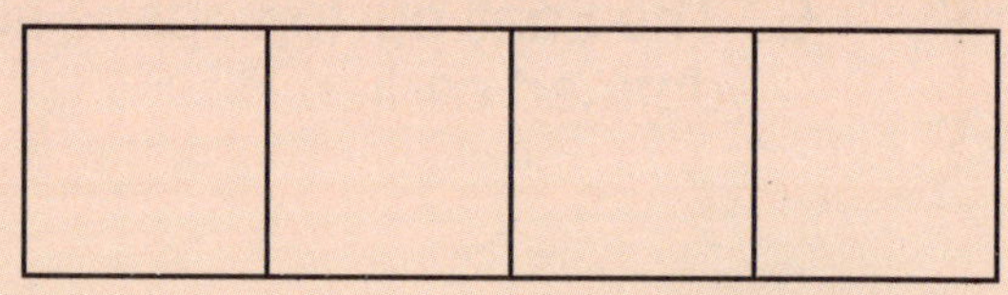

(**Hint**: Do not forget to use the command to hide the turtle. Write all the commands you have used.)

2. The adjacent output was produced using the MSWLogo command

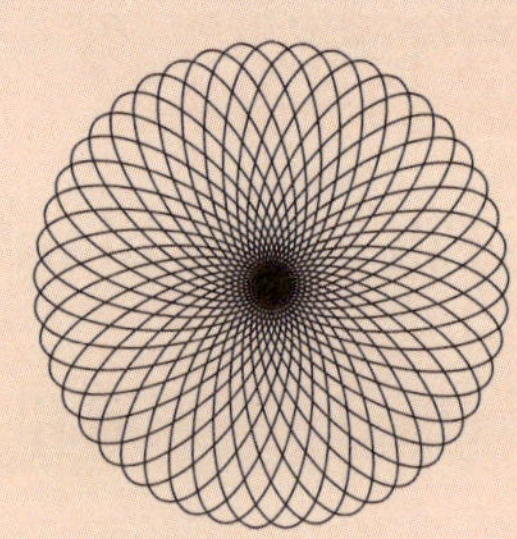

REPEAT 40 [REPEAT 360 [FD 1 RT 1] RT 10]

Define an MSWLogo procedure called SHAPE which would draw this shape as an output.

Now, use this procedure to produce the following output.

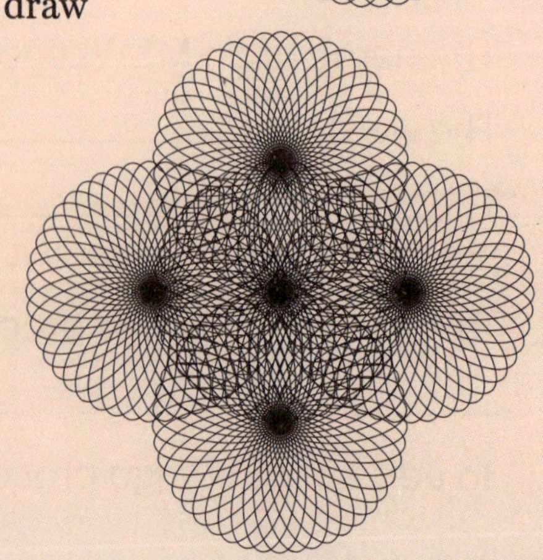

[**Hint**: You have to use the procedure SHAPE four times and use the PU and PD commands with the turtle movement commands (like FD, BK and HOME) to move the turtle to four different positions.]

FA

Research Project

Make a chart on the two ways of defining and editing procedures in MSWLogo. Make procedures to draw a regular octagon, a regular decagon and a circle. Name each procedure properly and save them.

Teacher's Note

Teachers should explain the concept of procedures with multiple examples, emphasizing the use of procedures inside other procedures or commands.

Also, demonstrate various methods to define and edit a procedure and encourage students to use the input box commands. Point out the proper syntax of the input box command, taking special care of the space and the double quote mark.

WORKSHEET

1. Write full form of the following:
   - MB • KB • TB • PB • GB

   Arrange these units in ascending order.
2. Which is the most suitable memory for storing the data permanently—primary memory or the secondary memory?
3. Can we group the bits in any other way other than the collection of 8 bits? What is the other possible combination and what is it called?
4. What are binary numbers?
5. Write the names of two types of ROMs. Also, write how they are different from each other.
6. Classify the following as primary memory devices or secondary memory devices.

(a) Pen Drive	(c) RAM	(e) CD
(b) DVD	(d) Hard Disk	(f) Floppy Disk

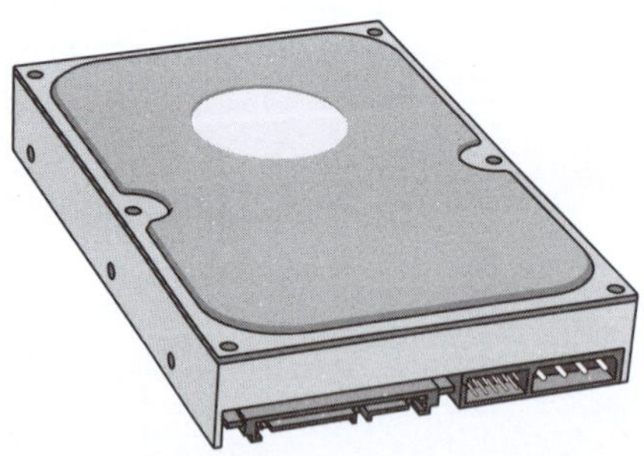

7. What are the storage capacities of CD, DVD and Blu-ray disc? Arrange the three in descending order of their storage capacities.
8. Write some examples of writeable and editable ROMs.

9. Look at the following flowchart. Can you tell what task this flowchart is performing?

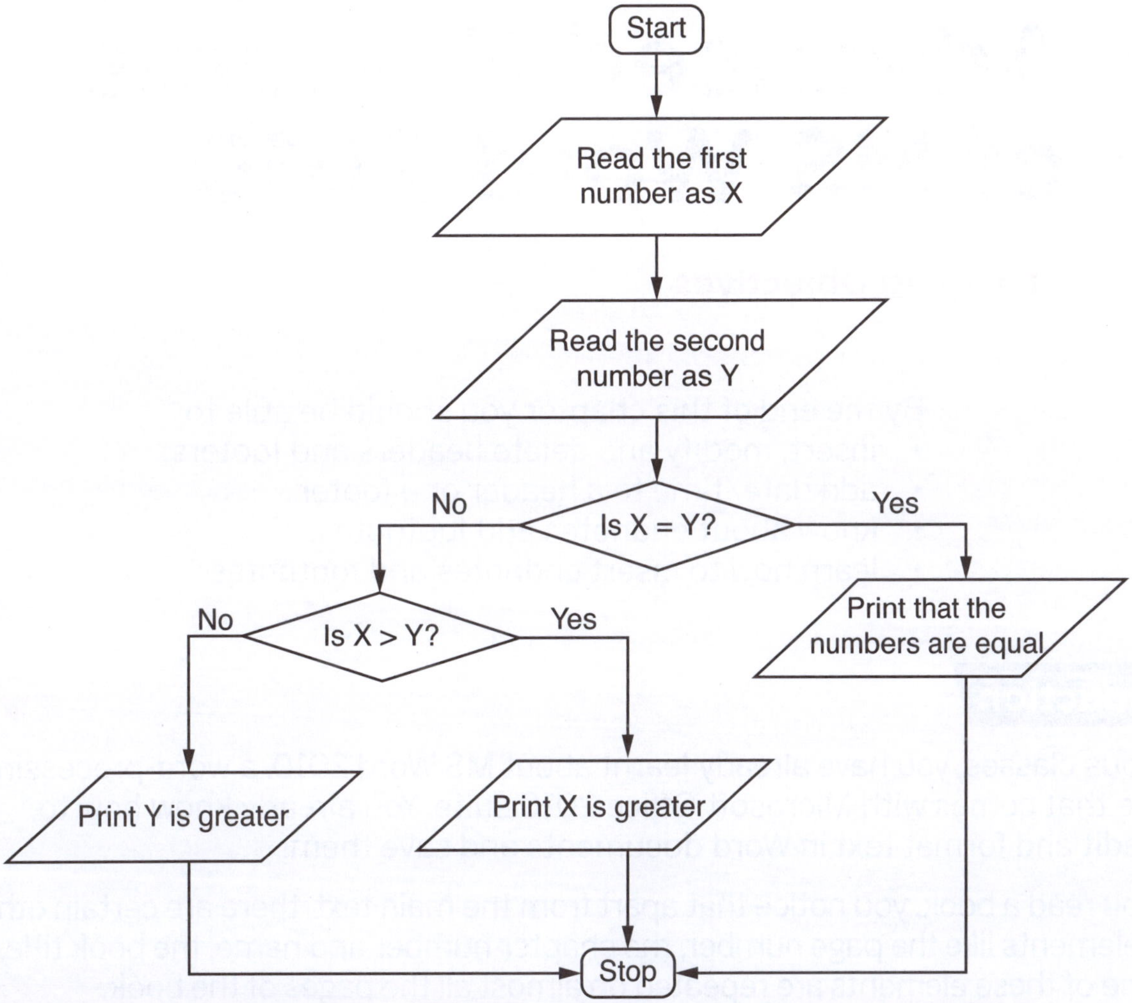

10. Design a flowchart similar to the one shown above to compare two negative numbers.

Projects

1. Do you remember MSWLogo command for drawing a circle? Define a procedure called CIRCLE which would draw a circle on the output screen.

   Now, can you use the procedure CIRCLE to produce the output shown in the figure?

   (**Hint**: Each time after drawing the circle, the turtle moves forward by 200 units and turns right by 90 degrees.)

   Write the commands you have used.

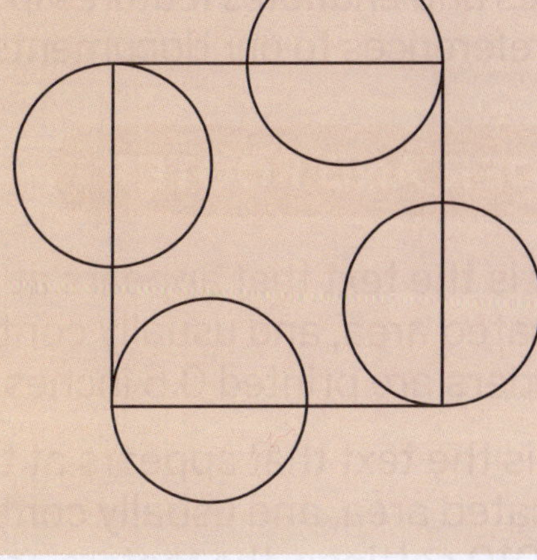

4 Advanced Features of MS Word 2010

Learning Objectives

By the end of this chapter you should be able to
- insert, modify and delete headers and footers.
- add date/time to a header or a footer.
- know about endnotes and footnotes.
- learn how to insert endnotes and footnotes.

Introduction

In previous classes, you have already learnt about MS Word 2010, a word-processing software that comes with Microsoft Office 2010 suite. You already know how to select, edit and format text in Word documents and save them.

When you read a book, you notice that apart from the main text, there are certain other textual elements like the page number, the chapter number and name, the book title, etc. Some of these elements are repeated on almost all the pages of the book.

MS Word allows you to add these textual elements to the Word document. It has certain predesigned features like **headers** and **footers** which help us add such information to the text.

Also, certain difficult words in some documents may have explanatory text as word meanings (usually in a smaller font size) at the end of the page, chapter or book. The footnotes and endnotes features in MS Word 2010 allow us to add such explanatory text or references to our documents. Let us study these elements.

HEADER AND FOOTER

Header is the text that appears at the top of a document page, in a specially demarcated area, and usually contains special text. By default, in MS Word 2010, the headers are printed 0.5 inches from the top of the page.

Footer is the text that appears at the bottom of a document page, in a specially demarcated area, and usually contains special text. According to the default MS Word 2010 settings, the footers are printed 0.5 inches from the bottom of the page.

Headers and footers are usually used when some information is repeated on multiple pages of a document. They contain special information such as document title, author's name, date or page number, etc. In addition, one can choose which information to put where.

In MS Word 2010, the options to insert and edit headers and footers are located on the **Insert** tab. (Fig. 4.1)

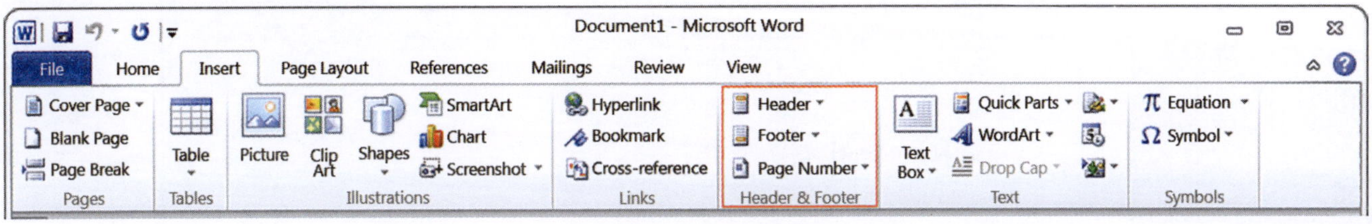

Fig. 4.1: Insert tab

You Should Know

You can see the headers and footers in a document only if you are in the **Print Layout** view. Otherwise, use the View Bar at the bottom right of the MS Word application window to select the **Print Layout** view.

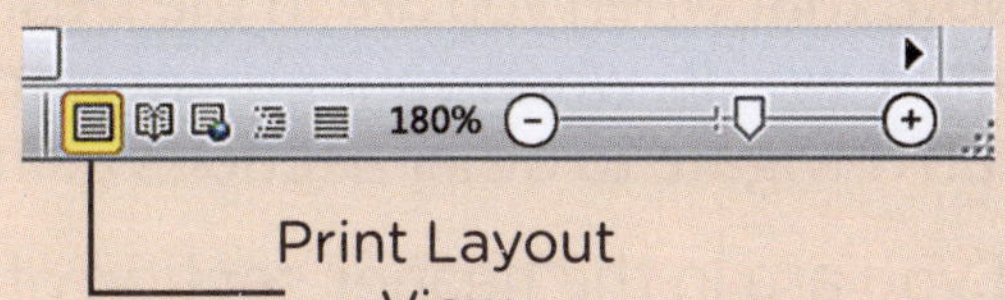

Inserting a Header or Footer

To insert a header or footer in a document, follow these steps:

1. On the **Insert** tab, in the **Header & Footer** group, click **Header** or **Footer** (Fig. 4.2).
2. This will open the **Header Gallery** or the **Footer Gallery** (Fig. 4.3), which gives you a variety of templates to choose from.
3. Select the **Blank** style if you want or scroll down the gallery to view further options.
4. This will open the **Design** tab under the **Header & Footer Tools** (Fig. 4.4). This tab is only visible when you have selected the header or the footer area of the document. Note that the **Title bar** changes to show that you are inside the **Header & Footer Tools** section. The cursor is also automatically placed in the header or footer section of the document and you can input any text you want. For example, the author's name or the title of the document can appear as the header or the footer.

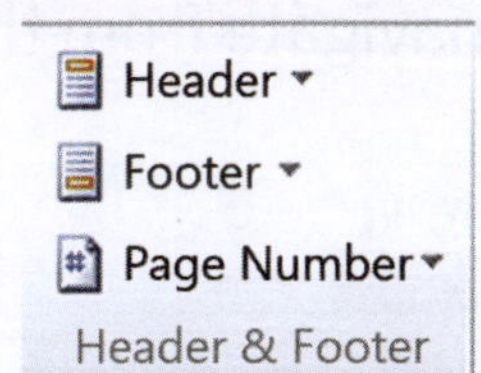

Fig. 4.2: Header & Footer group

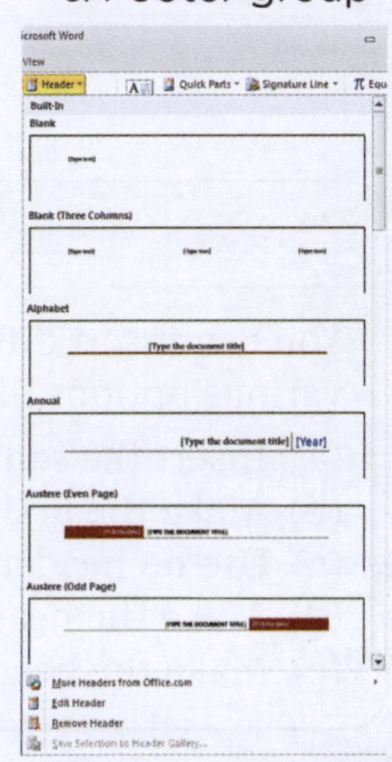

Fig. 4.3: Header gallery

5. Once you have finished inserting headers and footers, you can return to the main document by pressing the **Escape** key, or by clicking **Close Header and Footer** in the ribbon.

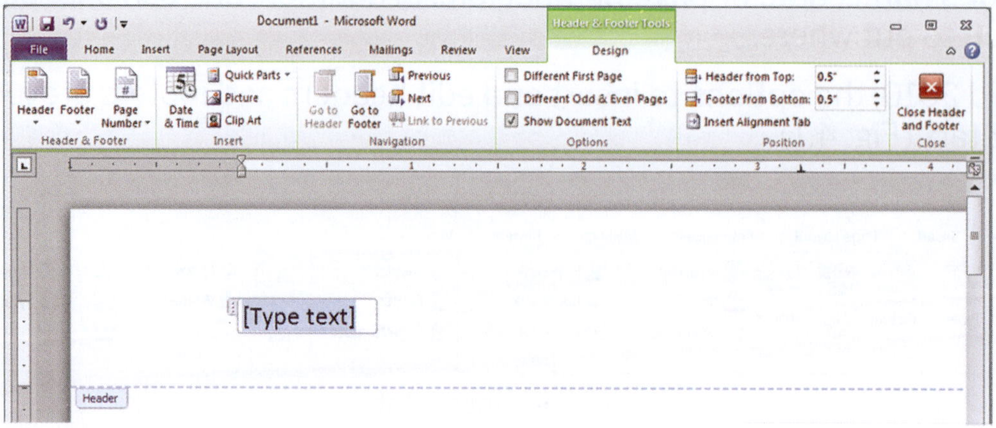

Fig. 4.4: Design tab under Header & Footer Tools

Note that when you are in the **Design** tab under the **Header & Footer Tools** (or in other words, when your cursor is in the header or footer section of the document), you can navigate to other sections using the **Navigation** group of buttons (Fig. 4.5).

If you are in the header section of the document, you can use the **Go to Footer** option to quickly navigate to the footer section of the document. Similarly, you can navigate from the footer to the header using the **Go to Header** option.

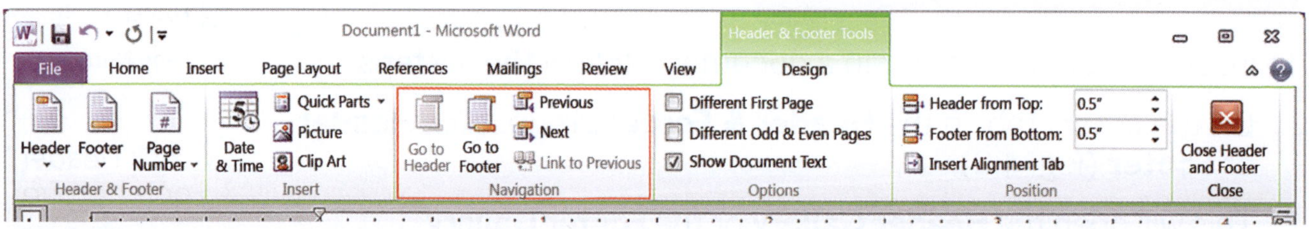

Fig. 4.5: Navigation group under Design tab

You Should Know

You can insert different headers and footers on different pages. MS Word 2010 offers us various options like:

(a) Insert the same header or footer on each page.
(b) Make the first page header or footer different from the rest of the pages.
(c) Use no header or footer on the first page.
(d) Make the header or footer different for odd and even pages.
(e) Make the header or footer different in each section or chapter.

Adding Date/Time to a Header or Footer

Apart from words, MS Word allows us to use the current system date and time as a header or footer. This feature is usually used to mark when the document was created. To do this, you have to follow these steps:

1. Select the header or footer by double-clicking on it. Note that the **Design** tab under the **Header & Footer Tools** (Fig. 4.4) opens automatically.
2. Click on **Date & Time** under the **Insert** group. (Fig. 4.6)

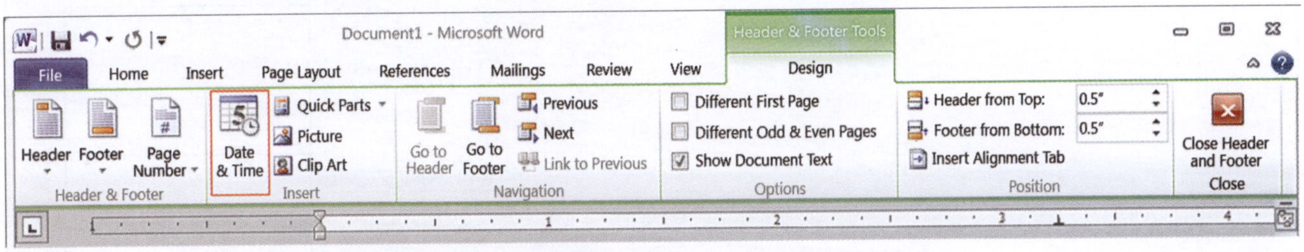

Fig. 4.6: Date & Time under the Insert group

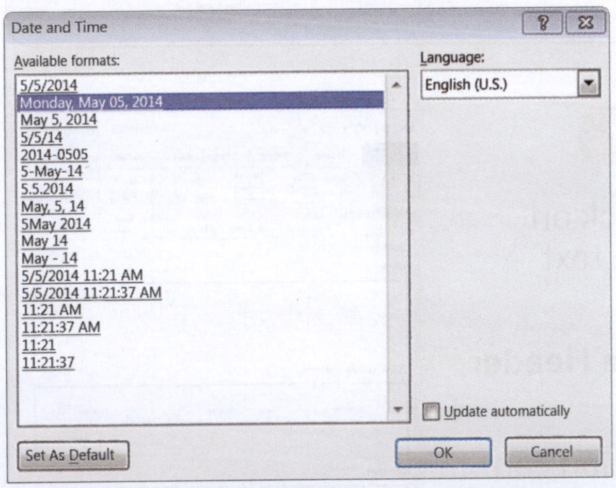

Fig. 4.7: Date and Time dialog box

3. This opens the **Date and Time** dialog box (Fig. 4.7).
4. Select a suitable date and time format to have it displayed with the selected header or footer (Fig. 4.8).

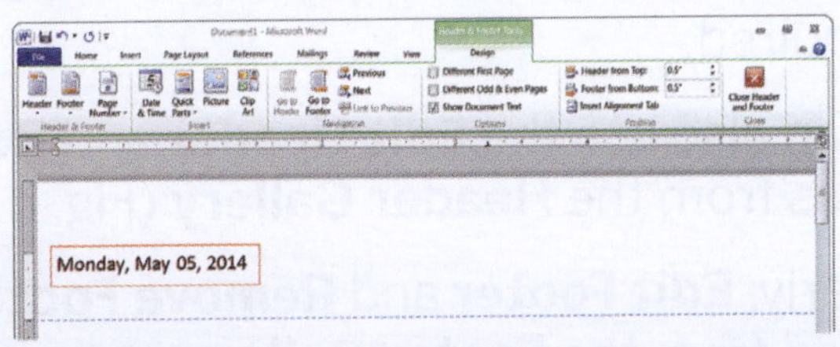

Fig. 4.8: Date displayed as header

5. Press the **Escape** key or click on the **Close Header and Footer** in the ribbon (Fig. 4.9).

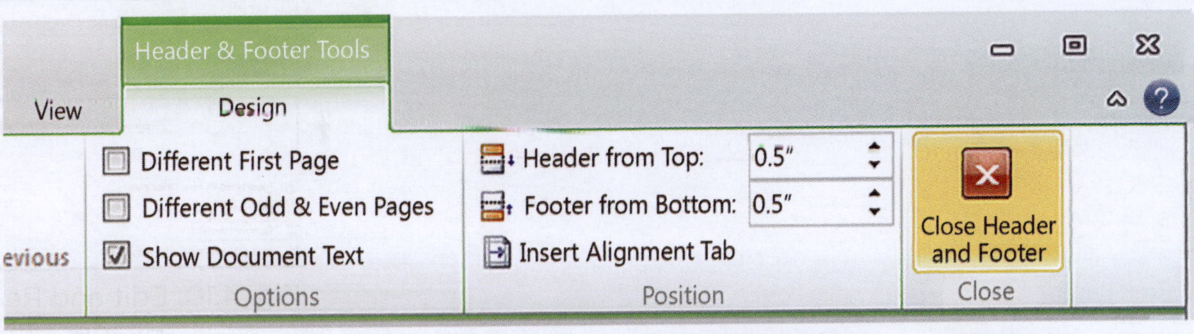

Fig. 4.9: Close Header and Footer

You Should Know

You can add page numbers to a document as header or footer by selecting the **Page Number** option in the **Header & Footer** group on the **Insert** tab and selecting the suitable option.

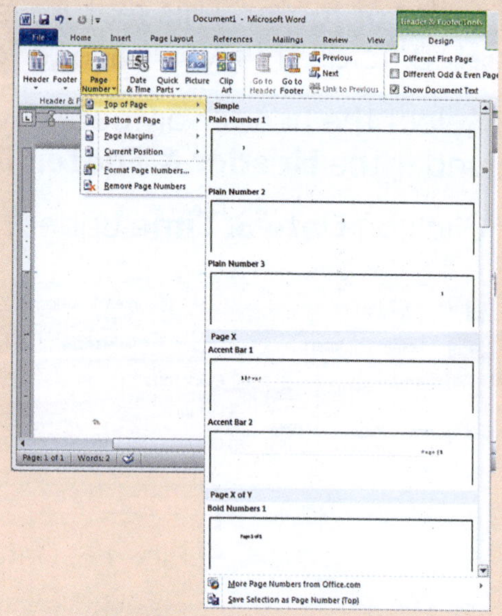

Editing and Deleting a Header or Footer

To edit or delete a header or footer, double-click on it to select it. You can simply edit or delete the text as required.

You can also use the **Edit Header** and **Remove Header** options from the **Header Gallery** (Fig. 4.10).

Similarly, **Edit Footer** and **Remove Footer** option can be used from the **Footer Gallery**.

Press the **Escape** key or click on the **Close Header and Footer** in the ribbon to exit and return to the main document.

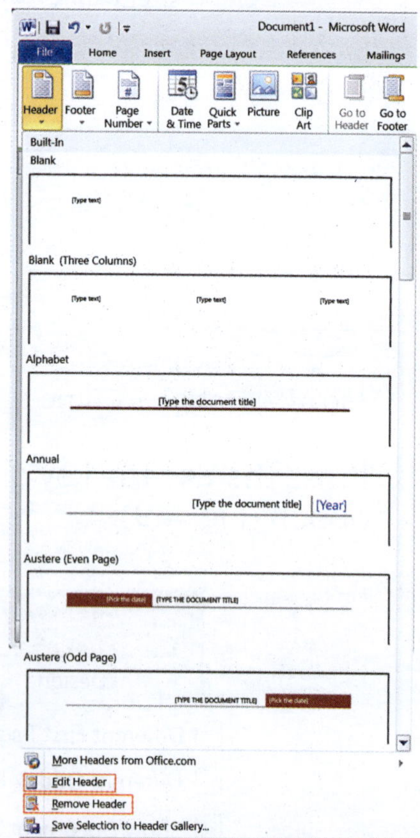

Fig. 4.10: Edit and Remove Header

FOOTNOTE AND ENDNOTE

Footnotes and endnotes are used in documents to explain, comment or provide references for text in a document.

Footnotes are placed at the end of the page in a document, whereas endnotes are placed at the end of a chapter, section or document.

A footnote or an endnote has the following parts (Fig. 4.11):

1. Footnote or endnote reference marks
2. Separator line
3. Footnote text
4. Endnote text

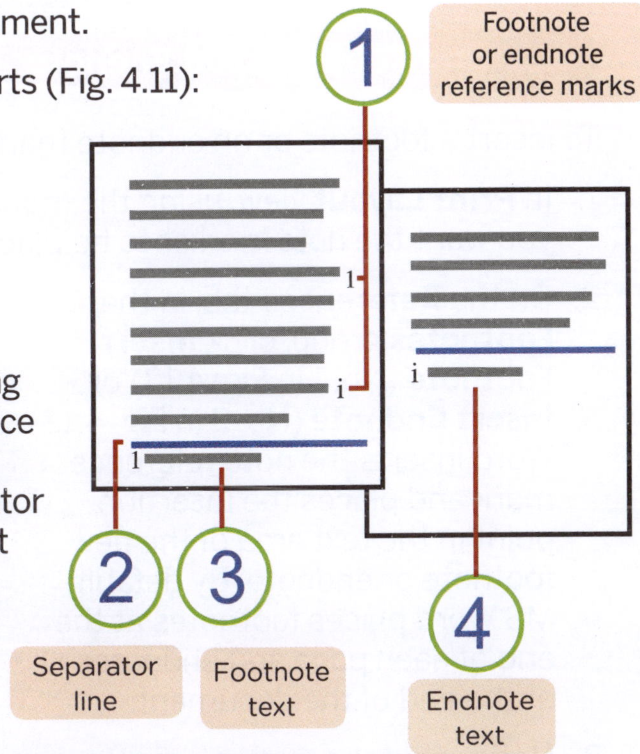

Fig. 4.11: Parts of Footnotes or Endnotes

The note reference mark and the corresponding note text are two linked parts. The note reference mark is placed next to the word or entry in the main text to be linked to the footnote. A separator line usually separates the body of the main text from the endnote or footnote section.

Footnotes are usually used for detailed comments and to add explanatory text. For example, while writing an essay on the development of computer over the ages, you might use the word ENIAC and link it to a footnote at the end of the page explaining what ENIAC is.

Endnotes are used for referring to sources which might have been cited in the main text. If you have used a quotation in your main text or have a reference in your text to some other document, you can add an endnote marker after the quotation or the reference and link it to a note at the end of the chapter/section/document mentioning the source document.

MS Word lets us add footnotes and endnotes to our documents as required.

Commands for inserting and editing footnotes and endnotes can be found on the **References** tab in the **Footnotes** group (Fig. 4.12).

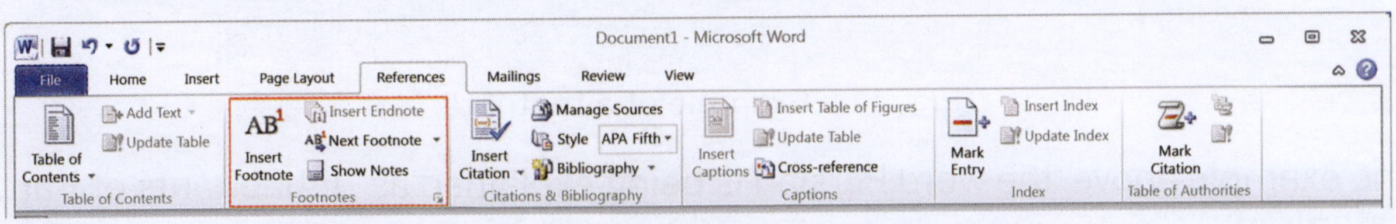

Fig. 4.12: Footnotes group on References tab

You Should Know

You can use numbers, letters, symbols or a combination of all of them as footnote or endnote markers. There can be a single numbering scheme throughout a document or you can use different numbering schemes within each section of a document.

Inserting Footnote and Endnote

To insert a footnote or an endnote marker after a word, follow these steps:

1. In **Print Layout** view, using the mouse or the arrow keys, bring the cursor where you want the note marker to be placed.
2. On the **References** tab, in the **Footnotes** group, click **Insert Footnote** (No. 1 in Fig. 4.13) or **Insert Endnote** (No. 2 in Fig. 4.13). Word inserts the note reference mark and places the insertion point in the text area of the new footnote or endnote. By default, MS Word places footnotes at the end of each page and endnotes at the end of the document.

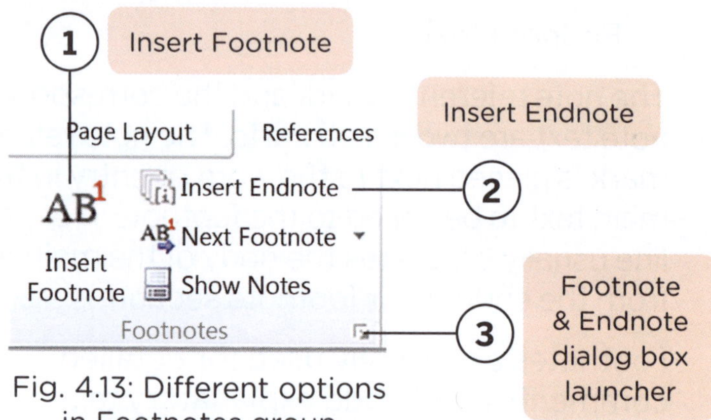

Fig. 4.13: Different options in Footnotes group

3. Notice that the cursor is on the footnote or endnote entry, next to the corresponding number at the end of the page/document. Enter the text you want as footnote or endnote. Remember, you can format this text in any way, so you can use different fonts and options like bold, italicize or underline.
4. Double-click the footnote or endnote reference mark to return to the reference mark in the document.

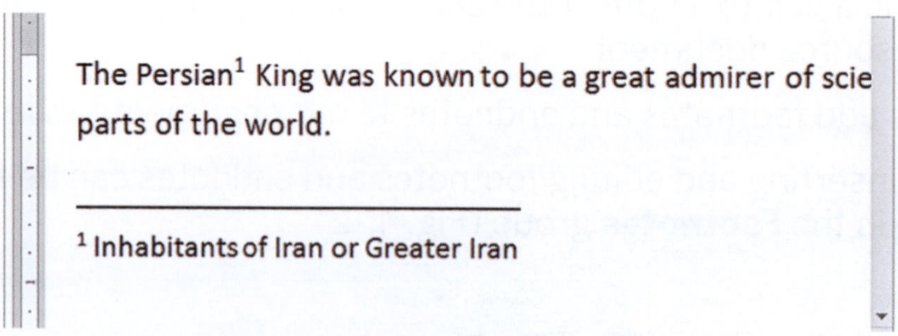

Fig. 4.14: Example of a footnote

In the example above, the word Persian is being explained as "Inhabitants of Iran or Greater Iran".

Quick Way

(a) To insert a footnote: Ctrl+Alt+F

(b) To insert an endnote: Ctrl+Alt+D

You Should Know

Clicking on the **Footnote and Endnote** dialog box launcher (No. 3 in Fig. 4.13) launches the **Footnote and Endnote** dialog box, which gives us the option to choose from a variety of settings for the footnote or the endnote like in the number format, where to start the numbering, whether the numbering is continuous or it restarts at each section/document. We can even use symbols as note reference markers by clicking on the **Symbol** button and choosing a suitable symbol from the **Symbol** dialog box. Click on **Apply** and then on **Insert** to add the selected footnote or endnote marker.

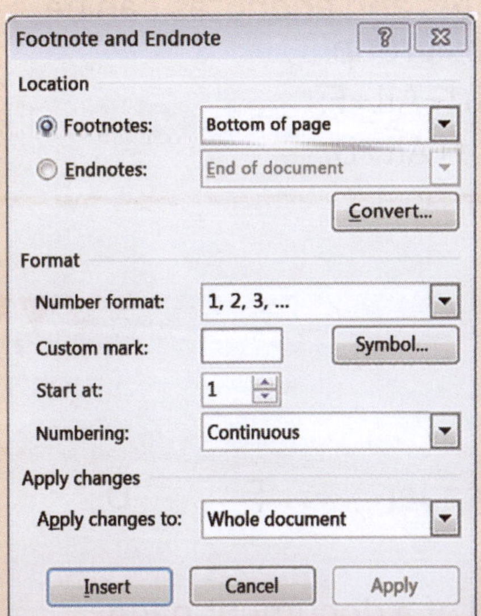

Practice Time

John was doing a project on *The Different Types of Data Storage Media.* He was writing a project report and had to use this title as a header on all the pages of the document. He also wanted to add the date as a footer on all the pages.

Write the steps for adding the header and footer.

John's report includes the word *binary*. He wants to add a footnote at the end of the page to explain what the word *binary* means. Write in steps how he can add the footnote.

Towards the end of the project, he wants to add an endnote mentioning all the websites he browsed to pick the images he used. Help him add endnotes for all the images he used.

Quick Recap

1. Headers and footers refer to the text that appear at the top and bottom of a document page, in a specially demarcated area, and usually contain special text like the document title, author's name, date and page number.
2. In MS Word 2010, the options to insert and edit headers and footers are present on the Insert tab in the Header & Footer group.
3. You can add page numbers or date and time as a header or footer.
4. To edit or delete a header or footer, double-click on it to select it. You can simply edit or delete the text as required.
5. Footnotes and endnotes are used in documents to explain, comment or provide references for the text in a document.
6. Commands for inserting and editing footnotes and endnotes can be found on the References tab in the Footnotes group.
7. Keyboard shortcut to insert a footnote is Ctrl+Alt+F.
8. Keyboard shortcut to insert an endnote is Ctrl+Alt+D.

EXERCISE

A Fill in the blanks using the words given below.

Footnotes Footer endnotes Header F D

1. ____________ is the text that appears at the bottom of a document page.
2. ____________ is the text that appears at the top of a document page.
3. ____________ are placed at the end of the page in a particular document whereas ____________ are placed at the end of a chapter, section or document.
4. To insert footnote, press Ctrl+Alt+ ____________ and to insert endnote, press Ctrl+Alt+ ____________.

B Write the steps for the following.

1. Inserting a footnote in MS Word 2010.
2. Inserting a header in MS Word 2010.

C Answer the following questions.

1. What is the difference between endnotes and footnotes?
2. Where do you find the option for adding headers and footers in MS Word 2010?
3. Can we replace endnotes by footnotes or footers? Why/Why not?
4. Can we insert page numbers as footers? How?

Lab Activity

FA

Start MS Word 2010. Write a paragraph on what MSWLogo procedures are and how to define them, using information from Chapter 3. Use a suitable title for your essay.

Insert the title of the document as the header on every page of the document and insert page numbers as footers.

Use a footnote to explain the term *Input Box* in your essay.

Save your document and exit MS Word.

Research Project

FA

Make a Word document tabulating the difference between primary and secondary storage using information given in Chapter 1.

Use the current system date as header and insert page numbers at the bottom right of the pages.

Use at least one instance of an endnote and one of a footnote to explain the terms you have used in the text. Use a symbol as the note reference marker.

Teacher's Notes

Teachers should show sample examples of the use of headers and footers, and endnotes and footnotes from different books.

Teachers can also demonstrate to students how footnotes and endnotes are linked using the note reference marks.

5 Mail Merge

Learning Objectives

By the end of this chapter you should be able to

- know what is Mail Merge and when do we use it.
- start Mail Merge.
- create a data source.
- add Merge Fields to the main document.
- merge the main document and the data.

Introduction

Subhash was preparing a surprise birthday party for his sister. He had already bought the gift and had planned where he was going to get the food from. The only thing that was now left was to send out the invitation letters. He had to send out invitations to at least 20 people. But Subhash was getting late for school and had no time to type out 20 invitation letters.

We might find ourselves in similar situations when we have to send a similar document to a large group of people. A survey form, an invitation letter, an office memo to be sent to all the office staff—all these are examples of such documents.

MS Word has a dedicated feature called **Mail Merge** which helps us to send personalized documents to a group of people without having to type each document separately. Mail merge allows us to create documents such that each document has similar information, but some content is unique. For example, in letters to his sister's friends, Subhash can personalize each letter to address a person by name. The unique information in each document comes from entries in the data source.

The Mail Merge process has the following general steps:

(a) **Setting up the main document**: The main document contains the text and graphics that are same in each version of the merged document. For example, the body of the invitation letter Subhash has to send.

(b) **Creating data source/Connecting the document to a data source**: A data source is a file that contains the information to be merged into a document. For example, the names and addresses of the 20 recipients of the invitation letter. MS Word also allows you to select and edit each recipient's details.

(c) **Adding placeholders, called mail merge fields, to the document**: When the Mail Merge is performed, the mail merge fields are filled with information from the data file. For example, to address each invitee by name, Subhash has to add a suitable merge field while writing the invitation letter. When performing the Mail Merge, each letter generated is addressed to each recipient.

(d) **Previewing and completing the merge**: Each copy of the document can be previewed before printing or emailing the whole set.

You use commands on the **Mailings** tab to perform a Mail Merge (Fig. 5.1).

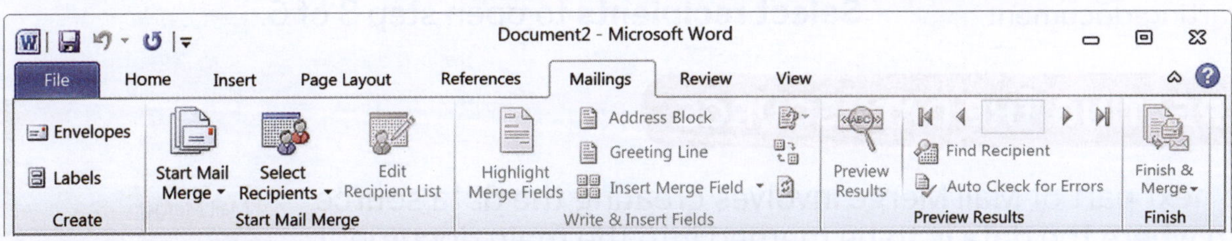

Fig. 5.1: Mailings tab

STARTING MAIL MERGE

To start Mail Merge and create the main document, follow these steps:

1. On the **Mailings** tab in the **Start Mail Merge** group, click **Start Mail Merge** (Fig. 5.2). In the menu that appears, note that **Letters** is the default document. Click on **Step by Step Mail Merge Wizard**.

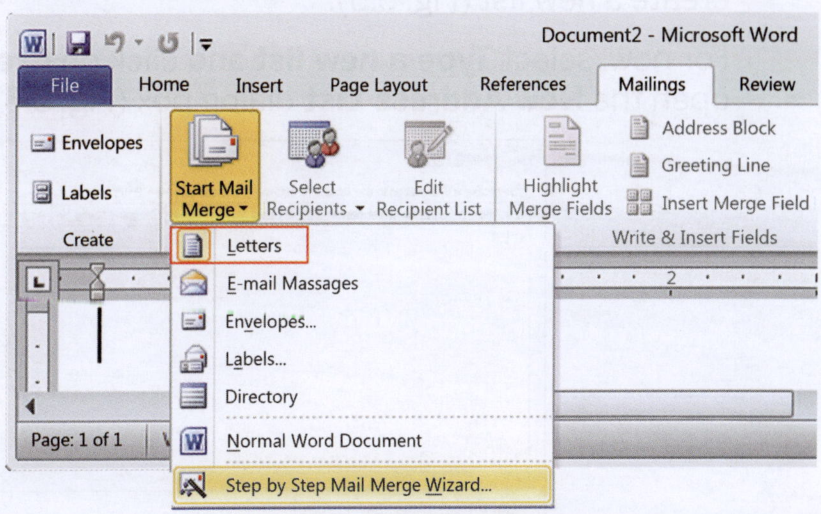

Fig. 5.2: Start Mail Merge

2. This opens the **Mail Merge** task pane to the right side of the MS Word application window.

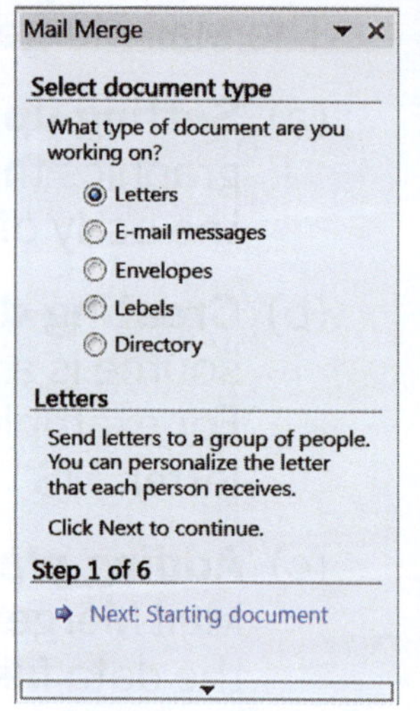

Fig. 5.3: Selecting the document type

Note that **Letters** is selected by default, as was indicated in the last step.

A small description is displayed when each of the options is selected. With **Letters** selected, click **Next: Starting document** (Fig. 5.3).

3. Step 2 of 6 is selecting a starting document. You can choose to use the document currently open by checking the option next to **Use the current document**.

   You can also use a template (by selecting **Start from a template**) or use an old document (by selecting **Start from existing document**) (Fig. 5.4).

   Select the current document for now and click on **Next: Select recipients** to open step 3 of 6.

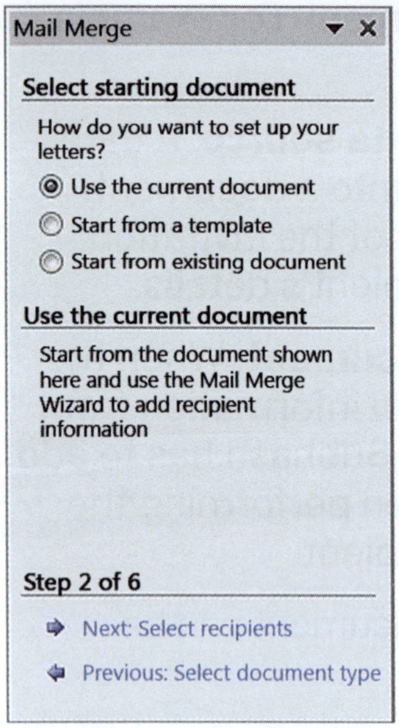

Fig. 5.4: Selecting a starting document

CREATING THE DATA SOURCE

The next part of Mail Merge involves creating the data source from where the data is to be merged into the main document.

4. Step 3 of 6 in the Mail Merge process is selecting the recipients. We can select the recipients either from an existing list or from the MS Outlook contacts or we can create a new list (Fig. 5.5).

   For now, select **Type a new list** and click on **Create** to open the **New Address List** dialog box (Fig. 5.6).

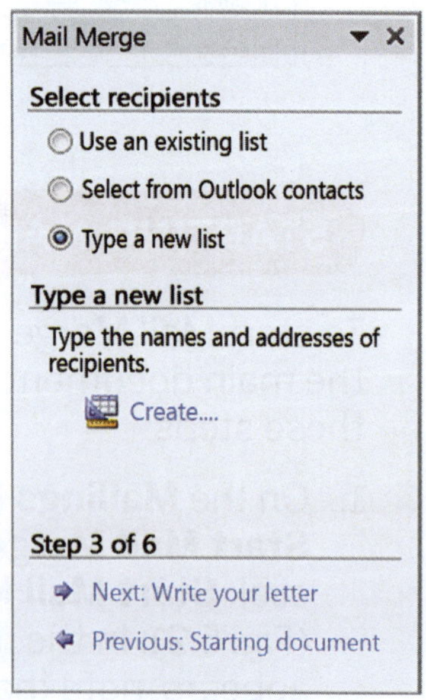

Fig. 5.5: Selecting recipients

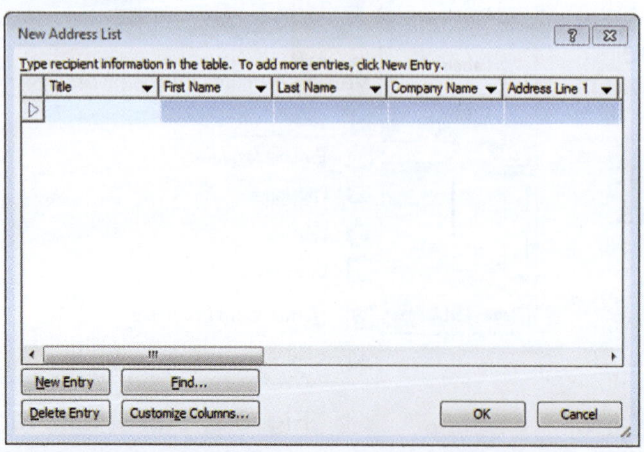

Fig. 5.6: New Address List dialog box

5. In the **New Address List** dialog box, click **Customize Columns** to open the **Customize Address List** dialog box (Fig. 5.7).

   You can rename any of the fields by selecting it and clicking on **Rename** or delete any field you might not require by selecting the field and clicking on **Delete** (note that you have to confirm the deletion).

   In Subhash's case, he only wanted the following fields—Name, Address Line 1, Address Line 2 and City.

   You can also add a field using the **Add** button.

   Click **OK** when you have made the necessary changes.

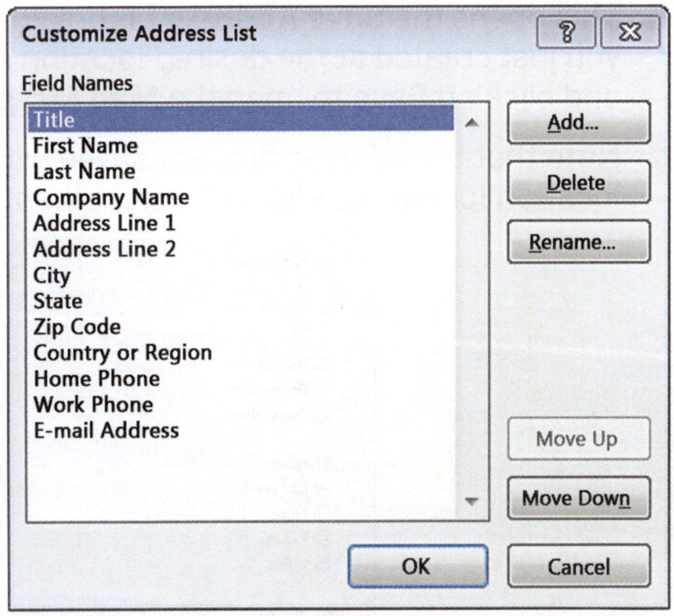

Fig. 5.7: Customize Address List dialog box

You Should Know

Microsoft Outlook is a personal email manager from Microsoft.

6. This takes you back to the **New Address List** dialog box, but this time it will show only the fields you had selected while customizing (Fig. 5.8).

   Use the **New Entry** button to enter new recipients. When you have entered the names of all the intended recipients, click **OK** (Fig. 5.9).

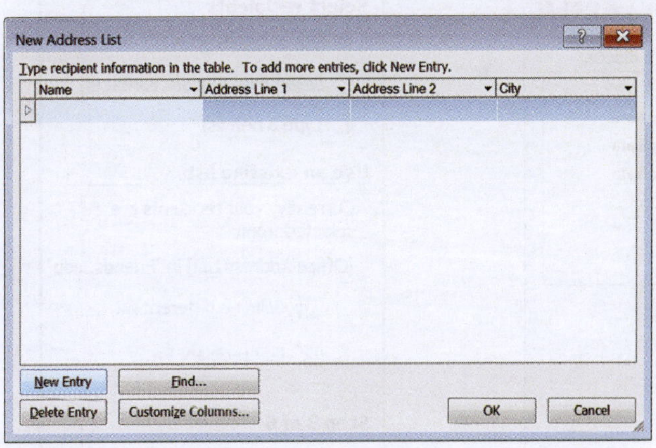

Fig. 5.8: New Address dialog box after customizing

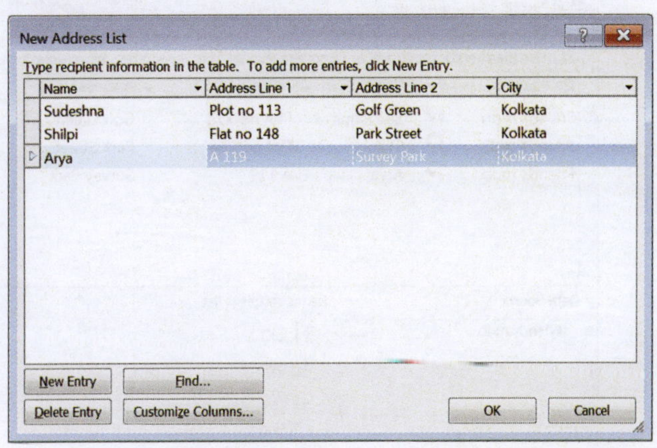

Fig. 5.9: New Address List dialog box with the list of recipients

7. This opens the **Save Address List** dialog box which allows you to save the list you just created at the desired location (Fig. 5.10). Choose a suitable file name and click on **Save** to open the **Mail Merge Recipients** window.

   Note that the address files are saved with an extension *.mdb*. The default location for saving a list is *My Documents\My Data Sources*.

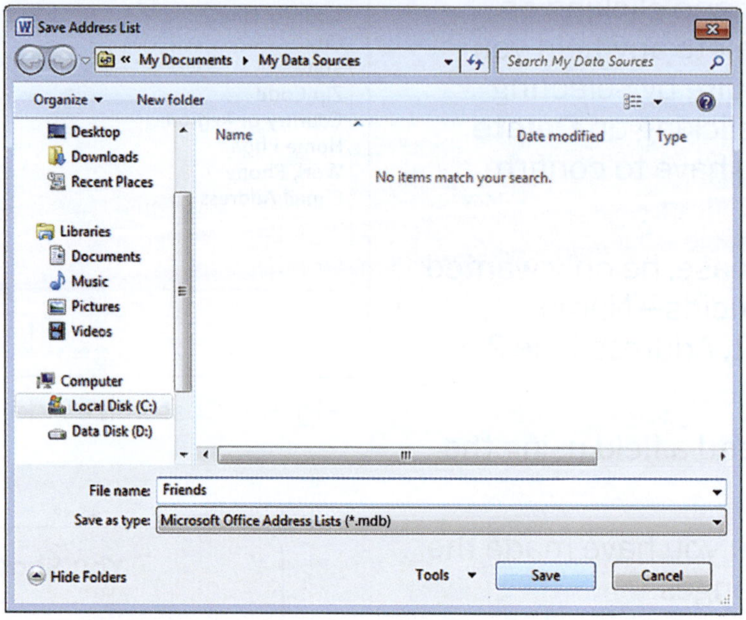

Fig. 5.10: Save Address List dialog box

8. The **Mail Merge Recipients** window allows you to see and edit the data you have already entered, and to select individual recipients (Fig. 5.11).

   When you are satisfied with the selection, click **OK** to close this window and return to Mail Merge step 3 of 6.

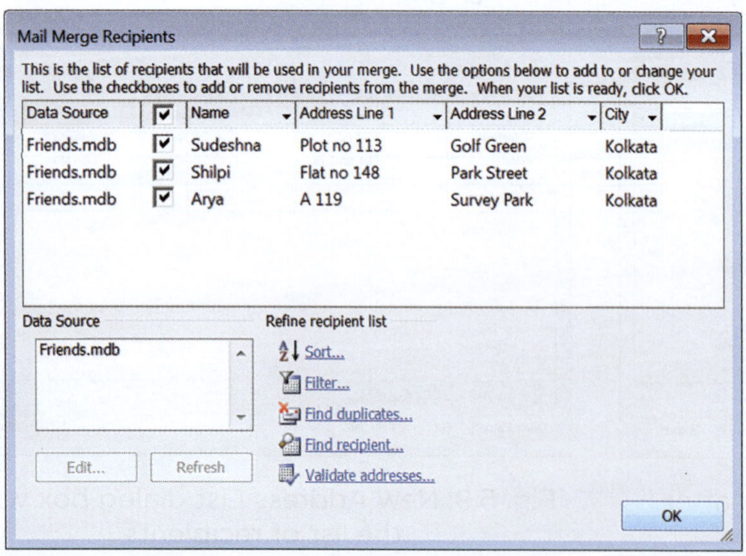

Fig. 5.11: Mail Merge Recipients window

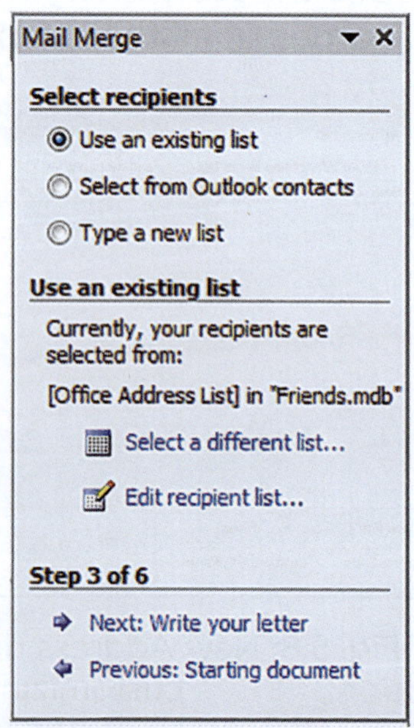

Fig. 5.12: Selecting recipients using an existing list

9. Now that you have a list of recipients to select from, in the **Mail Merge** task pane select the option **Use an existing list**.

   Click on **Next: Write your letter** (Fig. 5.12) to begin step 4 of 6.

ADDING MERGE FIELDS TO THE MAIN DOCUMENT

When finally the Mail Merge will be performed, the mail merge fields are filled with information from the list of recipients. Let us see how we can create a letter with embedded merge fields.

10. Type the letter and when you come to the section where you want to insert data from the data source, click on **More items** in the **Mail Merge** task pane (Fig. 5.13).

This will open the **Insert Merge Field** dialog box (Fig. 5.14).

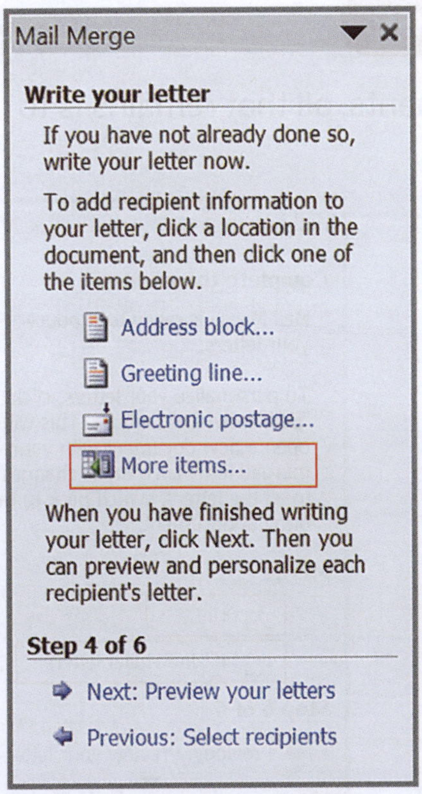

Fig. 5.13: Adding Merge Fields to the letter

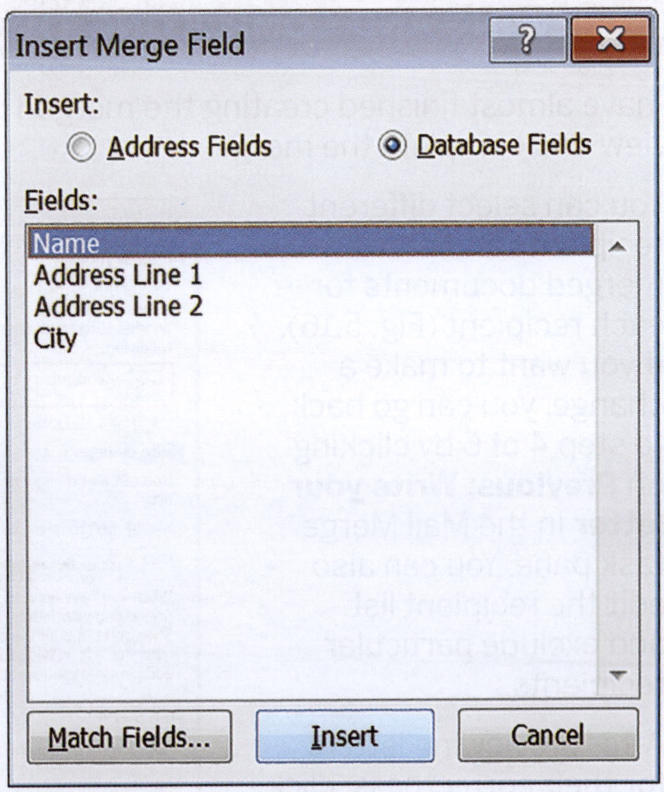

Fig. 5.14. Insert Merge Field dialog box

Select the field you want to use and click on **Insert** to add the merge field where your cursor is located (Fig. 5.14).

11. Type the letter, adding merge fields at suitable places until the letter is finished (Fig. 5.15).
12. Click on **Next: Preview your letters** when you finish typing to proceed to step 5 of 6.

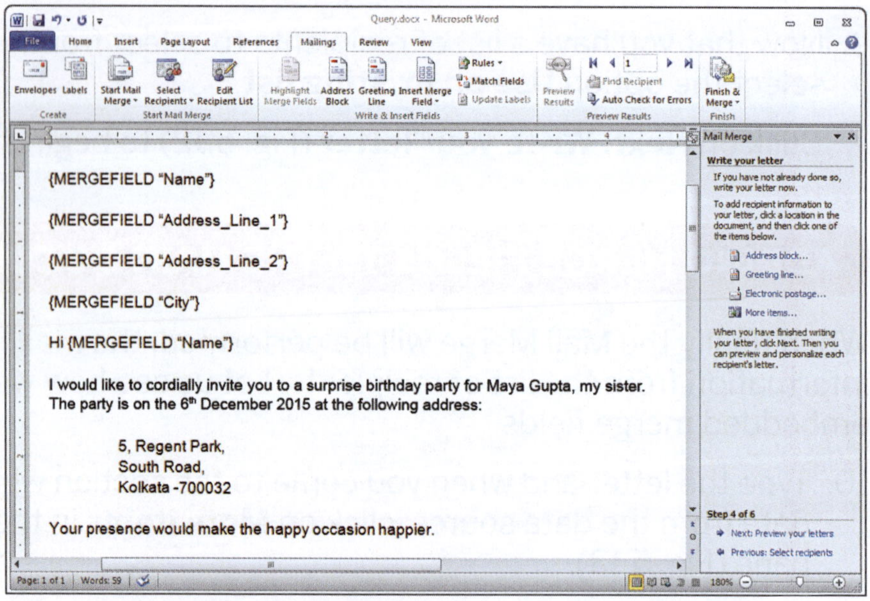

Fig. 5.15: An invitation letter with Merge fields

PREVIEWING AND COMPLETING THE MERGE

You have almost finished creating the merged documents, all that remains is to preview and complete the merge.

13. You can select different recipients and preview the merged documents for each recipient (Fig. 5.16). If you want to make a change, you can go back to step 4 of 6 by clicking on **Previous: Write your letter** in the Mail Merge task pane. You can also edit the recipient list and exclude particular recipients.
14. After previewing letters for their correctness, click on **Next: Complete the merge** to reach the last step 6 of 6.

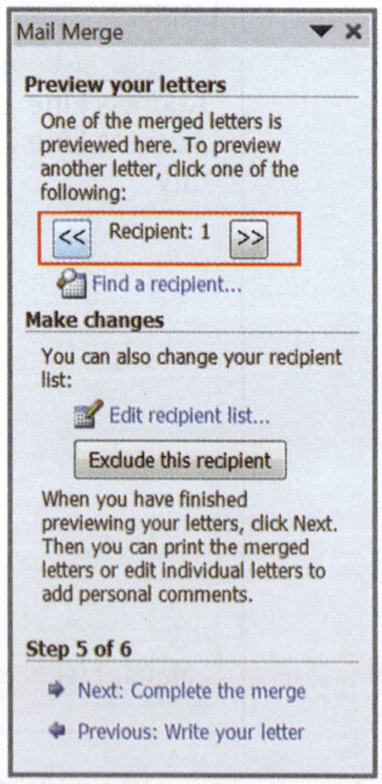

Fig. 5.16: Previewing the letters

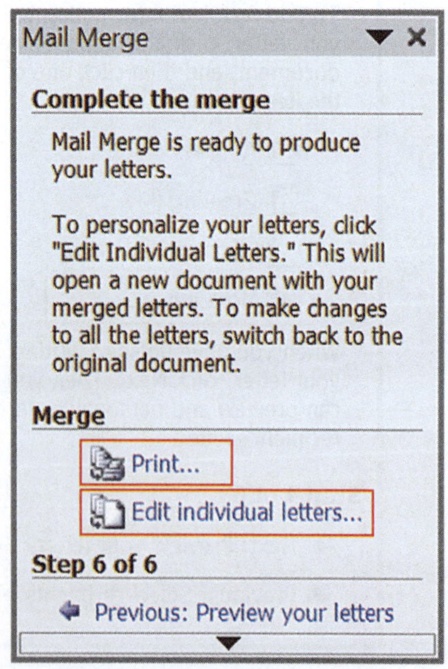

Fig. 5.17: Completing the merge

15. In the last step you can print all or some of the letters and even edit individual letters (Fig. 5.17).

In Fig. 5.18, you can see a merged letter. Note that the merge fields have been replaced with the recipient's details.

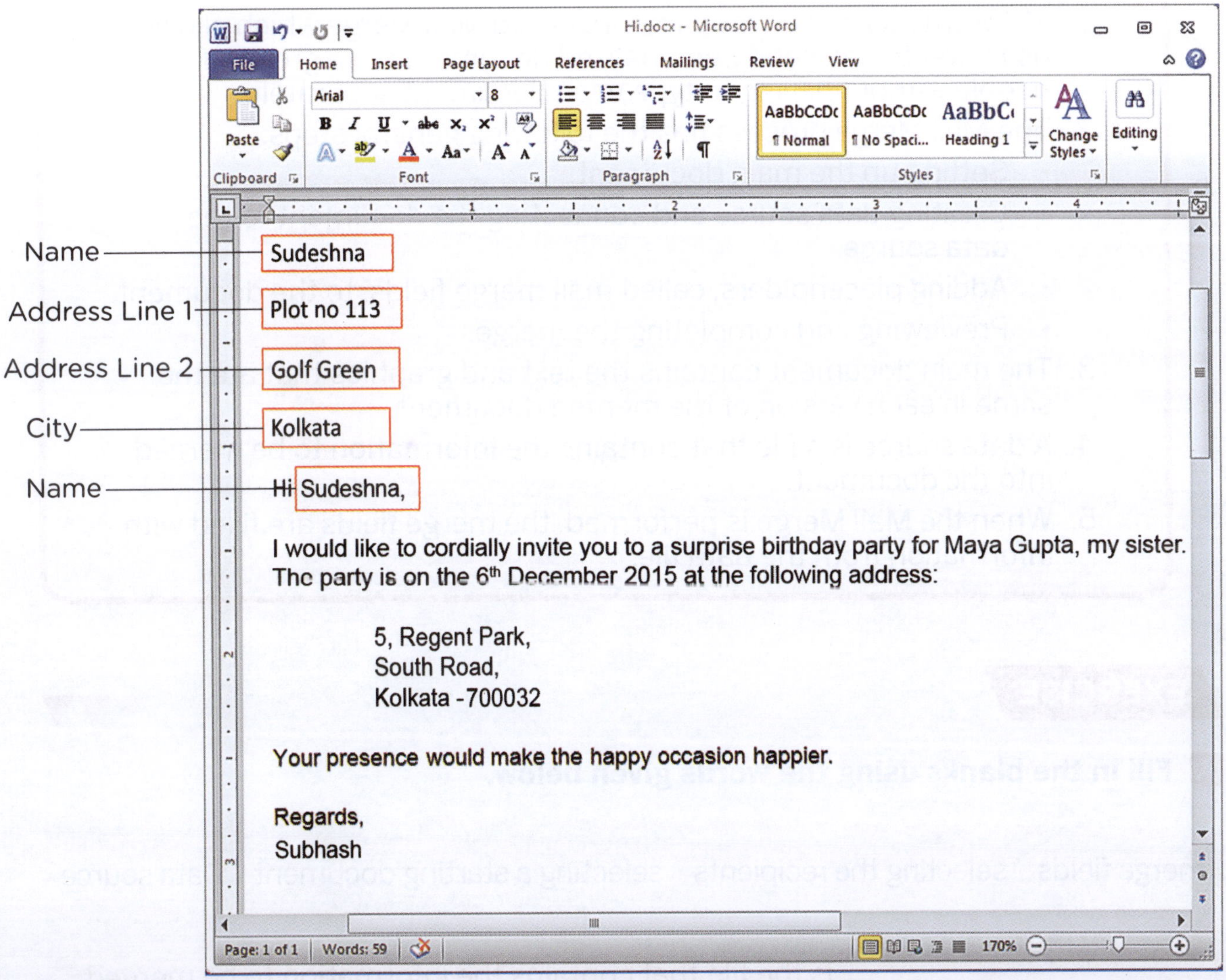

Fig. 5.18: A merged letter

Practice Time

Sameer has written a letter asking four of his friends—Arif, Gaurav, Sheela and Sonam—to come to his house for a party. He wants to send the same letter to everybody, except that he wants each letter to have his friend's name. Which MS Word feature can he use to compose the letters? Help him to compose the letter.

Now that you've helped Sameer with this task, list the benefits of using this specialized MS Word feature in your notebook.

Quick Recap

1. MS Word has a dedicated feature called Mail Merge which allows us to create and send personalized documents to a group of people without having to type each document separately.
2. The Mail Merge process has the following general steps:
   - Setting up the main document.
   - Creating data source and connecting the document to the data source.
   - Adding placeholders, called mail merge fields, to the document.
   - Previewing and completing the merge.
3. The main document contains the text and graphics that are the same in each version of the merged document.
4. A data source is a file that contains the information to be merged into the document.
5. When the Mail Merge is performed, the merge fields are filled with information from the data file.

EXERCISE

A Fill in the blanks using the words given below.

merge fields   selecting the recipients   selecting a starting document   Data source

1. ________________ is the file that contains the information to be merged into a document.
2. When the Mail Merge is performed, ________________ are filled with information from the data file.
3. Step 2 of 6 in the Mail Merge process involves ________________.
4. Step 3 of 6 in the Mail Merge process involves ________________.

B Write the steps involved in the following.

1. Inserting a merge field in the main document.
2. Creating a new address list.

C Answer the following questions.

1. When do we use Mail Merge?
2. What are the four basic parts of the mail merge process?
3. What is the main difference between a data source and the main document?

Lab Activity

FA

Start MS Word 2010. Use the Mail Merge feature to compose a letter on behalf of your school's drama club inviting five other schools to a theatre workshop in your school.

Your letter should include:

(a) Main body of the text inviting other schools.
(b) Names and addresses of the recipient schools at the top of the letter.

Research Project

FA

Can you think of two situations where Mail Merge will be useful?
Create a mail merge document for any situation. You may use one of the following hints or create your own situation.

- Seema is inviting five of her friends for a story-reading session.
- A teacher is sending out a report card to six of his students.

Teacher's Notes

Show sample examples of Mail Merge to make students conversant with the process so that they have a thorough understanding of how the information is being used from the data source in the main document to produce the merged document.

FA

WORKSHEET AND PROJECTS—2

WORKSHEET

A Unscramble the words and fill in the blanks.

1. You can see the headers and footers in an MS Word document if you are in the ______________ view. (TPINR TYAOLU)
2. On the Insert tab, in the Header & Footer group, click Header to open the ______________. (REEDHA YLLGARE)
3. You can add page numbers to a document as a header or footer by selecting the ______________ option in the Header & Footer group on the Insert tab. (EAGP RNEUMB)
4. Commands for inserting and editing footnotes and endnotes can be found on the ______________ tab in the Footnotes group. (RREEEESCFN)
5. You can use commands on the ______________ tab to perform a Mail Merge in MS Word. (IILNMAGS)

B State whether the following statements are true (T) or false (F).

1. Header is the text that appears at the top of a document page. ☐
2. When the Mail Merge is performed, the mail merge fields are filled with information from the main document. ☐
3. You cannot use numbers or symbols as footnote or endnote markers in MS Word. ☐
4. We cannot preview the merged letters. ☐

C What are the steps to perform the following actions in MS Word?

1. Inserting an endnote.
2. Editing or deleting a footer.

D Answer the following questions briefly.

1. What are the three main parts of a footnote or an endnote?
2. How do the contents of a main document and the data source vary?
3. How can you preview your merged letters?

E **The following screens are from the task pane on the right of the MS Word application window while performing a Mail Merge. Can you arrange them in the correct order?**

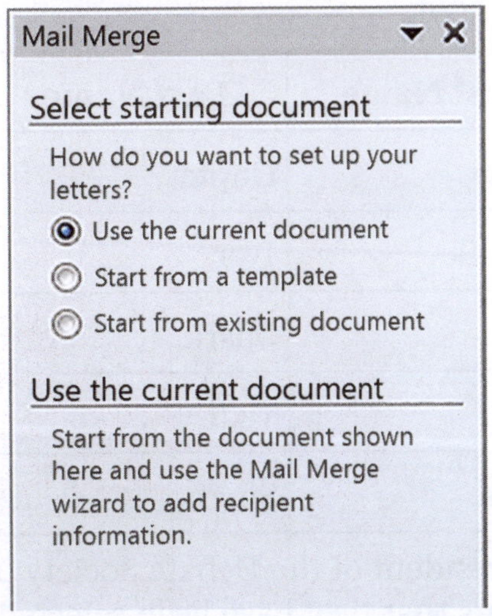

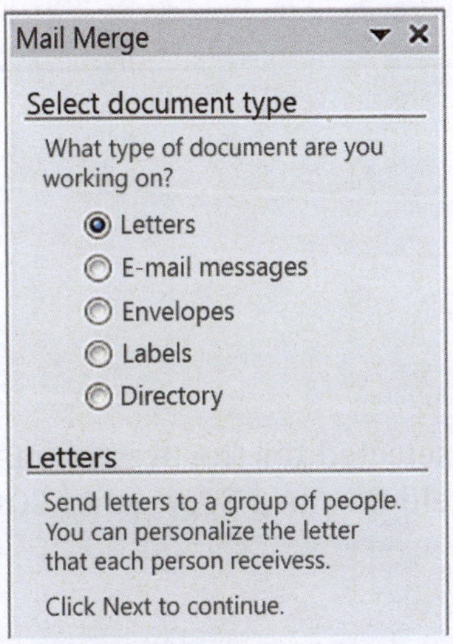

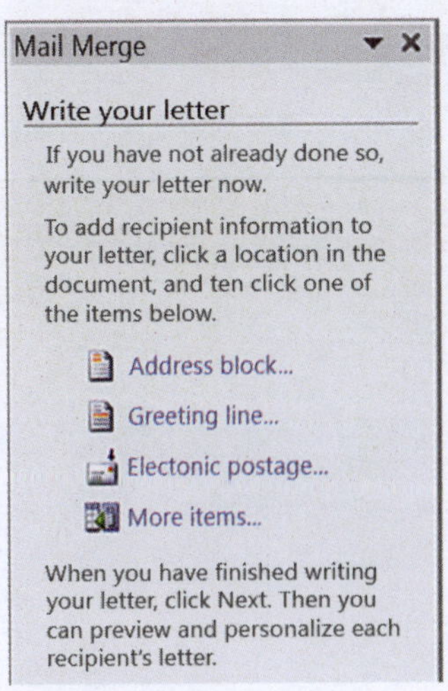

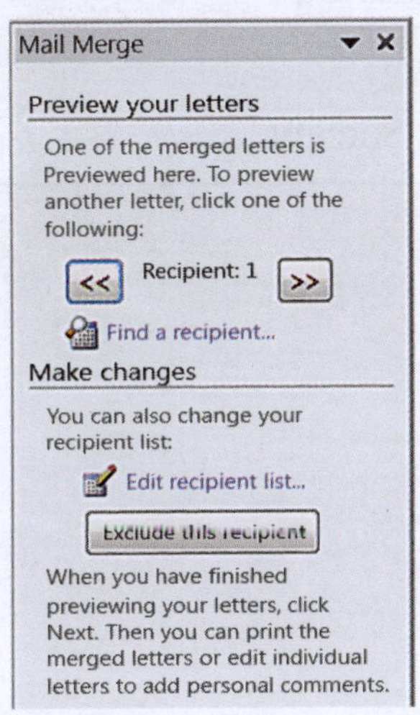

Projects

The following is a list of five students selected for the debate competition to be held in a school.

First Name	Last Name	Class	Roll No
Samir	Gupta	6	13
Kaushik	Iyer	5	2
Sonali	Misra	5	7
Sivesh	Vedi	7	2
Sakshi	Singh	6	10

The President of the Debate Society of your school needs to inform these five students that they have been selected for the competition. Which MS Word feature should he use? Can you help him compose the letter? One sample letter has been given as a clue.

Samir Gupta,

Class 6

Roll Number 13,

Dear Samir,

I am happy to inform you that you have been selected for the prestigious MK Gandhi Memorial Debate Competition to be held on the 3 September 2015.

Wishing you all the best,

Gaurav Sharma

President

Debating Society

6 Introduction to MS Excel 2010

Learning Objectives

By the end of this chapter, you should be able to
- start MS Excel.
- know the components of MS Excel.
- create a new spreadsheet.
- save a spreadsheet.
- open an existing spreadsheet.
- close a spreadsheet.

Introduction

We have already learnt about two important programs of the Microsoft Office software package—MS Word and MS PowerPoint.

A spreadsheet application is a computer program which has a number of inbuilt features and tools such as functions, formulas, charts and data analysis tools which help in doing the work with large amount of data easily.

Common spreadsheet programs include Microsoft Excel, OpenOffice Calc or Google Docs spreadsheets.

MS Excel is a spreadsheet program from the MS Office suite of programs. It can be used to create and format workbooks (a collection of spreadsheets) in order to analyze data and make more informed decisions on the basis of how the data is represented. MS Excel can be used to track data, write formulas to perform calculations on that data, build models for analyzing data, make tables from the data in different ways and present data in a variety of methods including charts and tables. The most recent versions of Excel are MS Excel 2010 and MS Excel 2013.

STARTING EXCEL

There are several methods to start MS Excel.

Fig. 6.1: Click on Start and then select All Programs

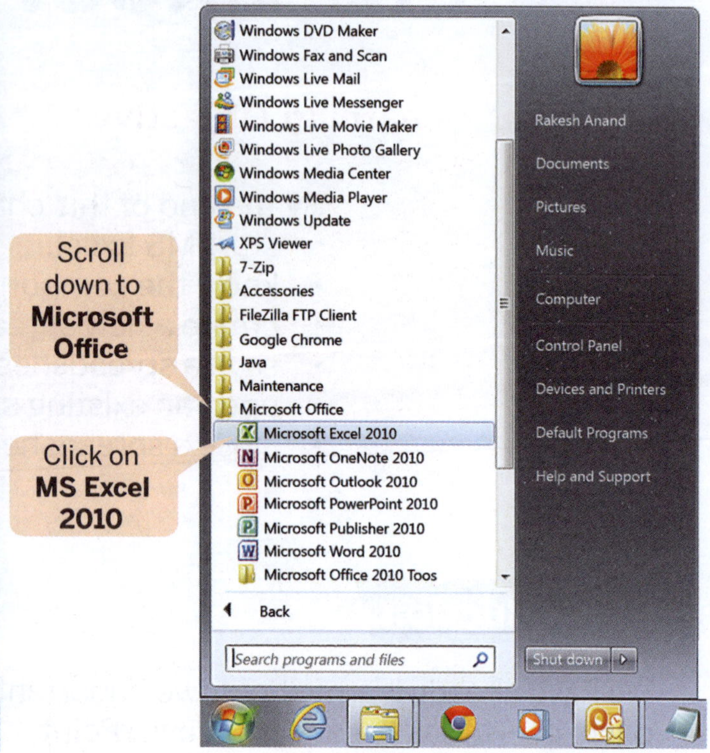

Fig. 6.2: Click on Microsoft Office and then select MS Excel 2010

To start MS Excel, follow the steps given below:

1. Click the **Start** button on your desktop (Fig. 6.1).
2. Click on **All Programs** (Fig. 6.1).
3. Scroll down until you find **Microsoft Office** and then click on it (Fig. 6.2).
4. Click on **Microsoft Excel 2010** (Fig. 6.2).

You Should Know

The default name given when a new workbook opens in MS Excel 2010 is *Book1.xlsx*.

Quick Way

1. On your keyboard, press the **Windows** key (⊞ key) and the letter **R** together. This opens the **Run** dialog box.
2. Type 'excel' and then click **OK**.

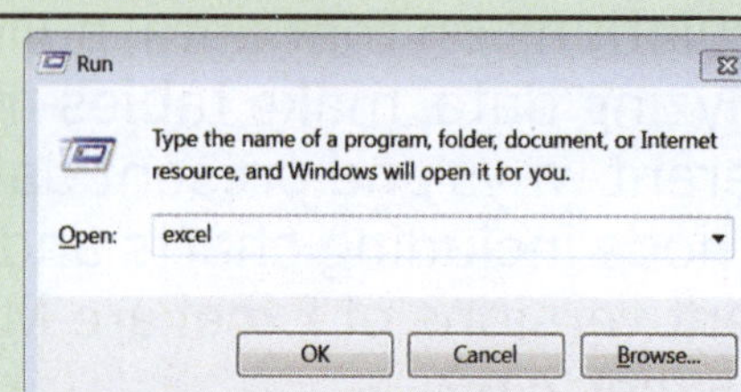

COMPONENTS OF MS EXCEL 2010

The various components of MS Excel 2010 application window are as follows:

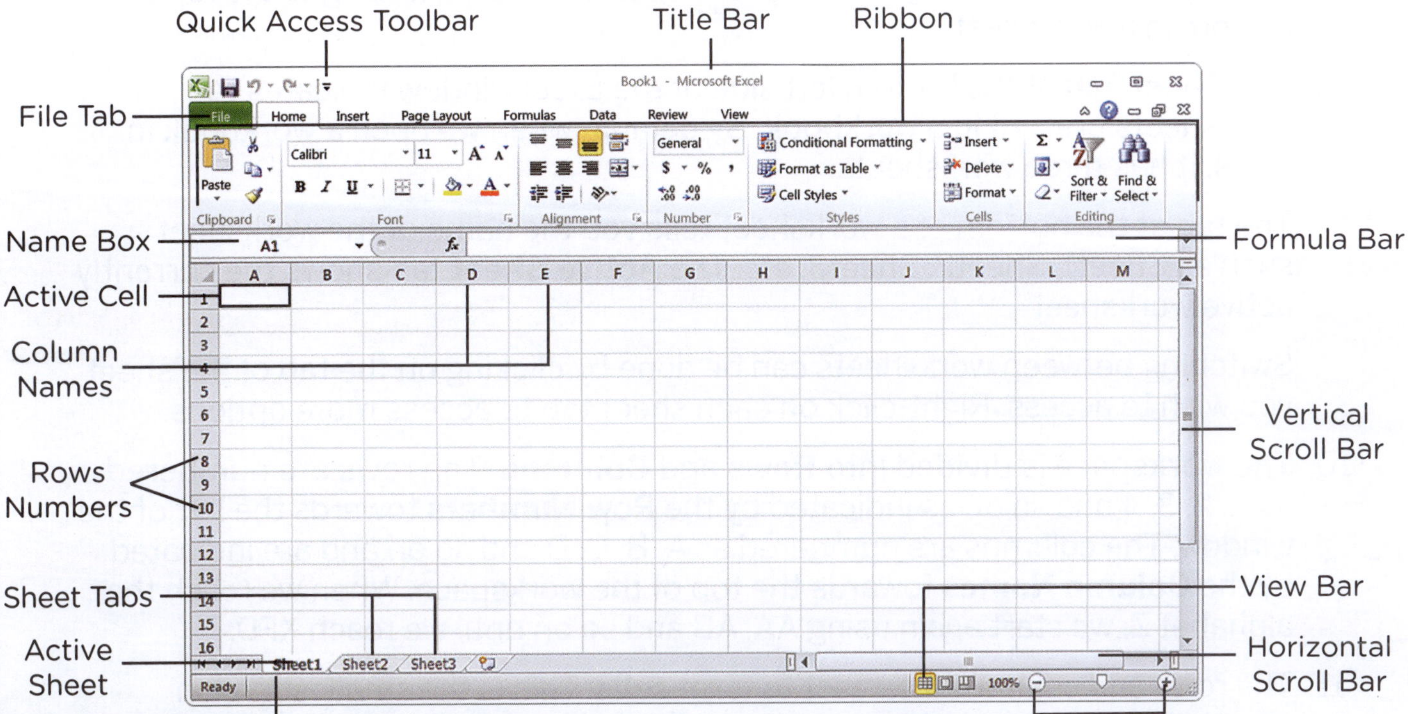

Fig. 6.3: Components of MS Excel 2010

1. The **Title Bar** is located at the top of MS Excel window. It displays the name of the workbook. The **Minimize**, **Maximize/Restore** and **Close** buttons are also located to the right of the title bar.
2. The **Quick Access Toolbar** contains some of the most frequently used commands like **Save**, **Undo** and **Redo**.
3. The **Ribbon**, which is present just below the title bar, contains different options grouped together as tabs.
4. The **File** tab present on the upper-left hand corner of the application window contains file handling options like **Save**, **Save As**, **Print**, **Close** and **New**.
5. The **Status Bar** which is present on the lower-left hand part of the application window shows status information like the current view, zoom tools, etc.
6. The **View Bar** is located in the lower right side of the application window and helps us to view the worksheets in different modes—the **Normal** view, the **Page Layout** view and the **Page Break Preview**.

7. The **Zoom Tools** located just to the right of the view bar allows the user to quickly set the zoom level of the document.
8. The **Horizontal Scroll Bar** helps the user to navigate left or right in a worksheet. A **Vertical Scroll Bar** may also be present which allows scrolling to the top or bottom in a worksheet.
9. The **Sheet Tab** at the bottom left side of the Excel window indicates the worksheets present in a workbook. By default, when we open a workbook in Excel, it has three worksheets.

   The tab at the bottom of a worksheet tells you the name of the worksheet such as Sheet1, Sheet2, Sheet3, etc. The **Active Sheet** tab shows the currently active worksheet.

   Switching between worksheets can be done by clicking on the tab of the sheet you wish to access. Right-click on each sheet tab to access more options.
10. The workspace is divided into **Rows** and **Columns**. The rows are numbered as 1, 2, 3, 4 and so on as indicated by the **Row Numbers** towards the left of the window. The columns are numbered as A, B, C, D and so on and are indicated by the **Column Names** towards the top of the workspace. When we reach the alphabet Z, we start again using AA, AB and so on until we reach XFD.
11. The rows and columns intersect to form **cells**. This is the smallest unit in a worksheet and can hold numbers, text or formula. Each cell has a unique address which is named as a combination of the row number and column name. Thus, the cell formed by the intersection of column C and 5th row has the address C5.
12. The **Active Cell**, as the name suggests, is the cell that is currently active or selected. It can be recognized by its thick black outline. Data is always entered into the active cell. Different cells can be made active by clicking on them with the mouse or by using the arrow keys on the keyboard.
13. The **Name Box** displays the cell reference or the address of the active cell. For example, in Fig. 6.3, the address of the active cell is A1.
14. Located above the workspace, the **Formula Bar** displays the contents of the active cell. It can also be used for entering or editing data and formulas in the active cell.

You Should Know

An Excel 2010 worksheet can have a maximum of 1,048,576 rows and 16,384 columns. Each cell can contain a maximum of 32,767 characters.

CREATING A NEW WORKBOOK

When MS Excel is started, by any of the two methods described earlier, the application window opens with a new workbook, containing three worksheets by default.

However, to open a new workbook when the MS Excel application is already running, follow the steps given below:

1. Click on the **File** tab in the MS Excel 2010 window. (Fig. 6.4)
2. Click on **New**.

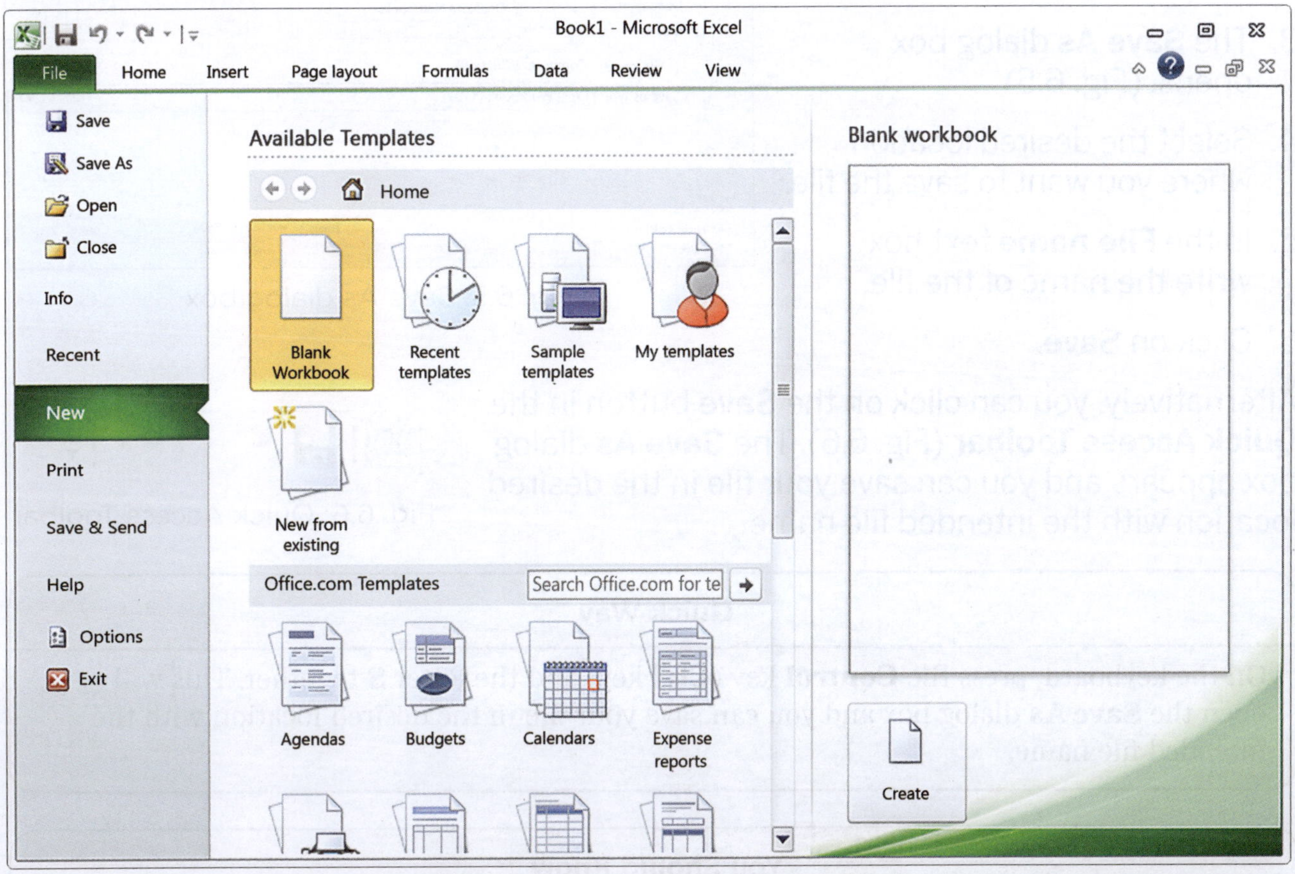

Fig. 6.4: Select Blank Workbook

3. Double-click on **Blank Workbook** or choose an existing template to open a new workbook.

Quick Way

With the MS Excel application open, press the Control key (**Ctrl** key) and the letter N together. This will open a new workbook.

SAVING A WORKBOOK

Once you have finished using a workbook, you would want to save the file. Follow the steps given below to save a workbook:

1. Click on the **File** tab in the MS Excel 2010 window.
2. Click on **Save**.
3. The **Save As** dialog box opens. (Fig. 6.5)
4. Select the desired location where you want to save the file.
5. In the **File name** text box, write the name of the file.
6. Click on **Save**.

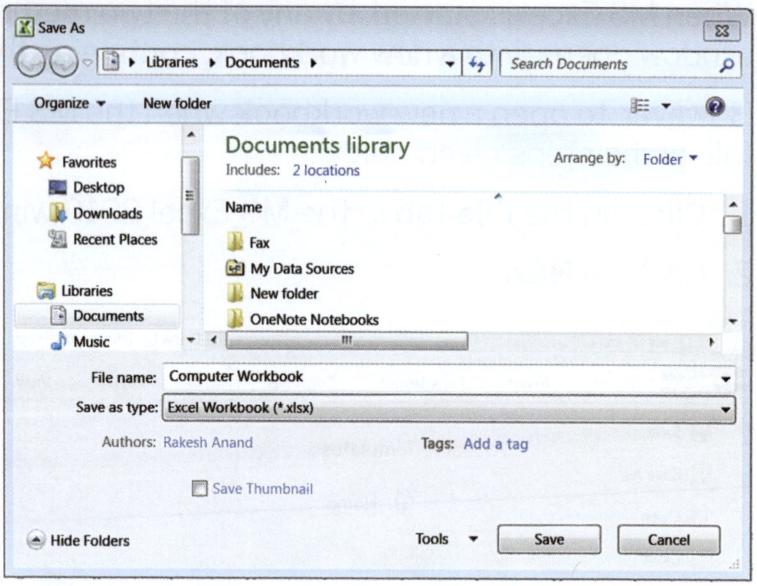

Fig. 6.5: Save As dialog box

Alternatively, you can click on the **Save** button in the **Quick Access Toolbar** (Fig. 6.6). The **Save As** dialog box appears and you can save your file in the desired location with the intended file name.

Fig. 6.6: Quick Access Toolbar

Quick Way

On the keyboard, press the **Control** key (**Ctrl** key) and the letter **S** together. This will open the **Save As** dialog box and you can save your file in the desired location with the intended file name.

You Should Know

- The **Save As** dialog box appears only the first time the Save option is used after the file is created. After that, the **Save** option does not open this box and automatically saves over the older workbook. In order to save another copy of the same file (at a different location or with a different name), click on the File tab and then choose the **Save As** option.
- The recent versions of MS Excel (2007, 2010 and 2013) add a period (full stop) and an extension *xlsx* after the file name. So, an MS Excel document with the name *computers* will have a complete file name as *computers.xlsx—computers* is the file name and *.xlsx* represents the file extension, which is specific to the type of file. The earlier versions of Excel used the extension *xls*.

OPENING AN EXISTING WORKBOOK

When MS Excel is not running, we can open an Excel workbook by browsing to the folder which contains the document file and then double-clicking on it.

However, if an MS Excel 2010 application window is already open, one can open an existing file by following any of the methods described below.

1. Click on the **File** tab.
2. Click on **Open**.
3. The **Open** dialog box opens (Fig. 6.7).
4. Browse to the folder where the MS Excel file you want to open exists.
5. Select the file you want to open. If you have selected the file, the name of the file will be displayed in the **File name** text box.
6. Click **Open** so that the workbook gets displayed in the application window.

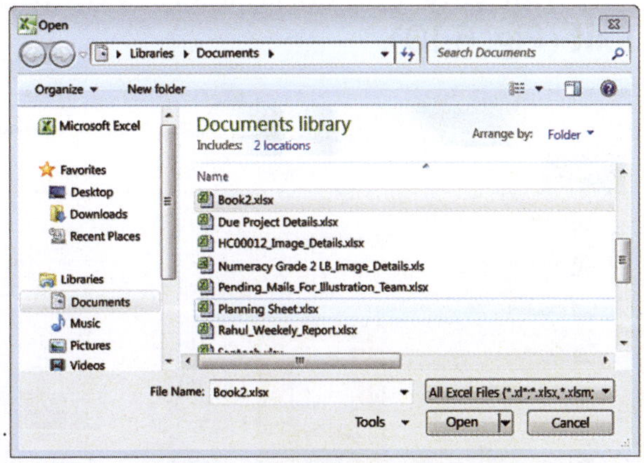

Fig. 6.7: Open dialog box

Quick Way

On the keyboard, press the Control key (**Ctrl** key) and the letter **O** together. This will open the **Open** dialog box and you can open your file by following the steps 4 to 6 as described above.

CLOSING A WORKBOOK

When we want to close a particular workbook in MS Excel 2010, but not the application window, we click on the **File** tab and then on **Close** (Fig. 6.8).

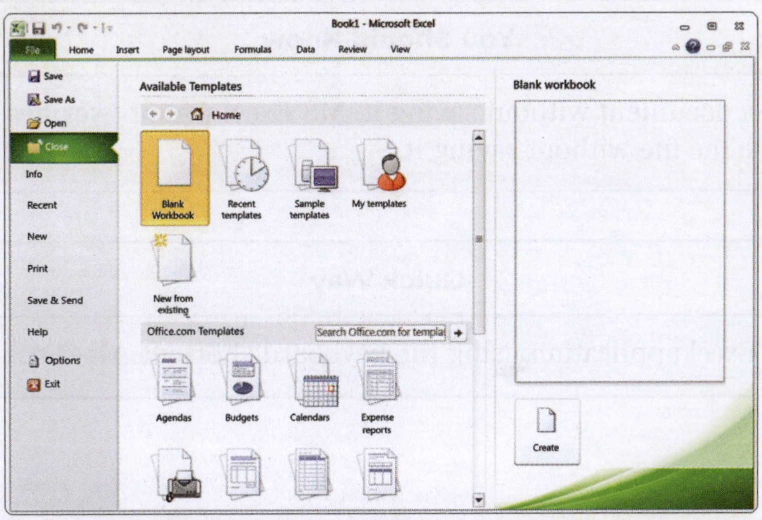

Fig. 6.8: Click on File tab and select Close

To exit the MS Excel application, click on the **Close** button to the top right of the application window (Fig. 6.9).

Fig. 6.9: Close button

Alternatively, you can click on **File** tab and then on **Exit** (Fig. 6.10).

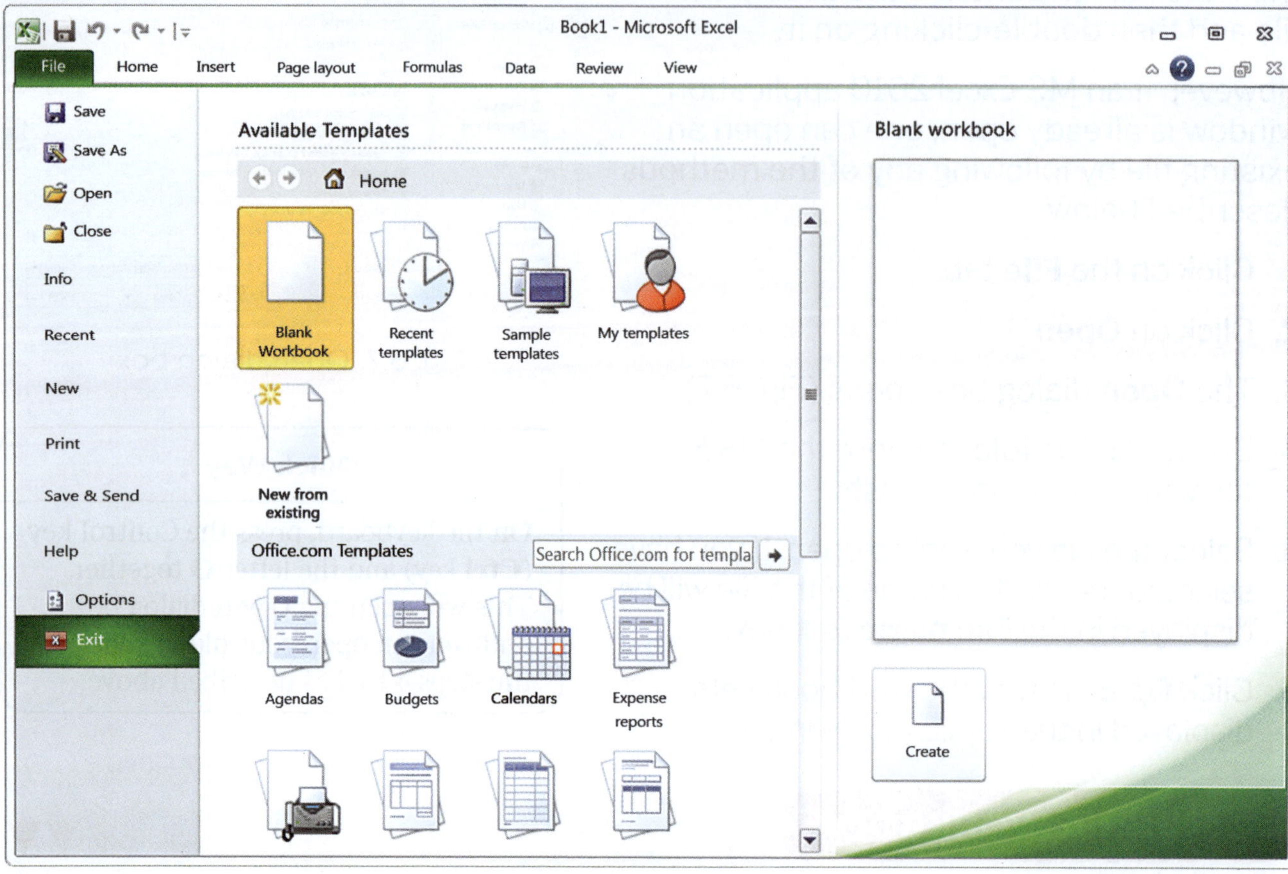

Fig. 6.10: Select Exit

You Should Know

If you try to close a document without saving it, MS Excel prompt verifies whether you really want to close the file without saving it.

Quick Way

You can close MS Excel application using the keyboard shortcut **Alt+F4**.

Quick Recap

1. MS Excel is a part of the Microsoft Office suite of programs. It can be used to create and format workbooks (a collection of spreadsheets) in order to analyze data and make more informed decisions on the basis of how data is represented.
2. To start Excel 2010, click on Start ▶ All Programs ▶ Microsoft Office ▶ Microsoft Excel 2010.
3. Some of the important components of the MS Excel 2010 application window are the title bar, formula bar, rows and columns, name box, File tab, ribbon and status bar.
4. By selecting the required option from the File tab, we can open new and existing files and save the files.
5. We can click on the Close button to exit the MS Excel 2010 program.
6. MS Excel 2010 files are saved with the extension *.xlsx*.
7. The following are some important keyboard shortcuts for MS Excel:
   - Ctrl+S   to save a workbook
   - Ctrl+N   to open a new workbook
   - Ctrl+O   to open an existing workbook
   - Alt+F4   to exit the MS Excel application

EXERCISE

A Fill in the blanks using the words given below.

rows   *.xlsx*   title bar   Book1   columns

1. The name of workbook is displayed in the ________________.
2. The ________________ are numbered as 1, 2, 3 and so on, while the ________________ are numbered as A, B, C and so on.
3. MS Excel 2010 files have the extension ________________.
4. The default name for a workbook is ________________.

B Write the keyboard shortcuts for the following in MS Excel 2010.

1. Opening Excel using the Run dialog box
2. Saving a workbook
3. Opening a new workbook
4. Opening an existing workbook

C Describe the following terms briefly.

1. Cell
2. Active Cell
3. Rows
4. Columns
5. Sheet Tab
6. Formula Bar

D Point out the various components of the MS Excel application window in the following screen.

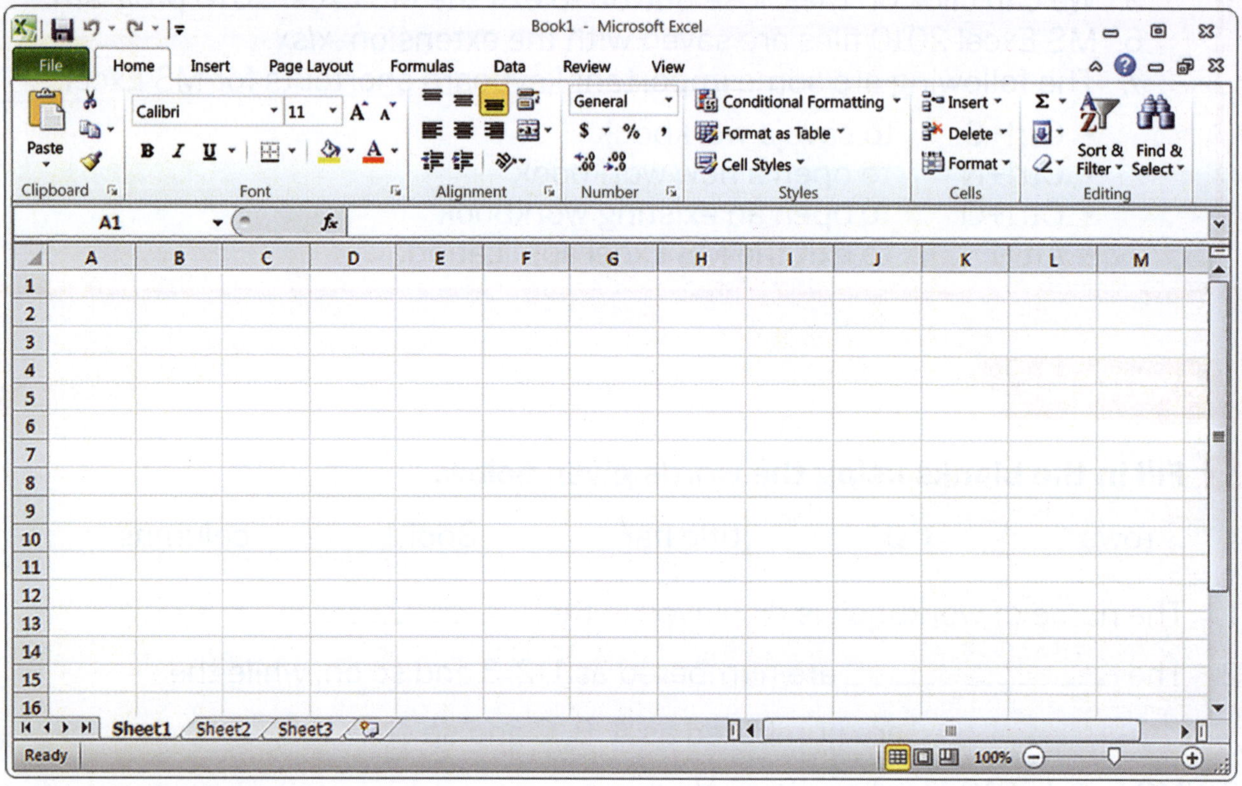

E Answer the following questions.

1. Describe two different methods of opening an existing workbook in MS Excel 2010.
2. Which is the smallest unit of a worksheet? Where can we see its address?
3. What are rows and columns in MS Excel? How are they numbered?
4. Describe the steps for saving a workbook in MS Excel 2010 using the File tab.

5. What will be the address of the following cells:
   a. Formed by the intersection of the row 16 with column H.
   b. Formed by the intersection of column B and row 135.

Lab Activity

FA

Start MS Excel 2010 using the Start menu. Write down the steps you have followed.

Now, make an Excel file showing some major countries in the world with their capitals. Refer to the adjacent figure.

Save the workbook as *Capitals*. Write down the steps involved in saving the file.

Close the application. Which method did you use to close it?

What is the full name of the file you saved? (Do not forget the extension.)

	A	B
1	Argentina	Buenos Aires
2	Australia	Canberra
3	Austria	Vienna
4	Bangladesh	Dhaka
5	Bhutan	Thimphu
6	Brazil	Brasília
7	Canada	Ottawa
8	China	Beijing
9	Colombia	Bogotá
10	France	Paris
11	Germany	Berlin
12	Greece	Athens
13	India	New Delhi

Research Project

FA

1. Try to think of five situations where we might use an Excel sheet to analyze or represent data.

Teacher's Notes

Demonstrate opening, closing and saving files on MS Excel 2010 with their keyboard shortcuts.

Also, introduce students to the basic text formatting options in Excel (like bold, italicized or underlined text, increasing/decreasing font size, etc.) as these formatting actions are already known to the students from MS Word 2010 chapters.

7

Adding Features to a Presentation

Learning Objectives

By the end of this chapter you should be able to
- enliven a PowerPoint presentation using pictures, screenshots, Clip Art, shapes and SmartArt.
- create a photo album using MS PowerPoint.
- use audio and video in presentations.

Introduction

We have already learnt that Microsoft Office software package includes the program MS PowerPoint to help us display information in an organized and systematic way. MS PowerPoint is a visual and graphical application primarily used for creating computer-based presentations.

We know how to start MS PowerPoint, how to create a new presentation or open an existing one, how to add new slides to a presentation and how to save a presentation.

Practice Time

Do you remember the keyboard shortcuts to do the following in a PowerPoint file?

1. Saving a presentation
2. Opening a new presentation
3. Exiting the PowerPoint application
4. Opening an existing presentation
5. Adding a new slide

PowerPoint 2010 is a presentation software that allows us to create dynamic slide presentations. While making a presentation in PowerPoint, one can create, view and present slide shows that combine text, shapes, pictures, graphs, animation, charts, sounds, videos and much more. The **Insert** tab in MS PowerPoint has the options for adding various objects to enhance a presentation (Fig. 7.1).

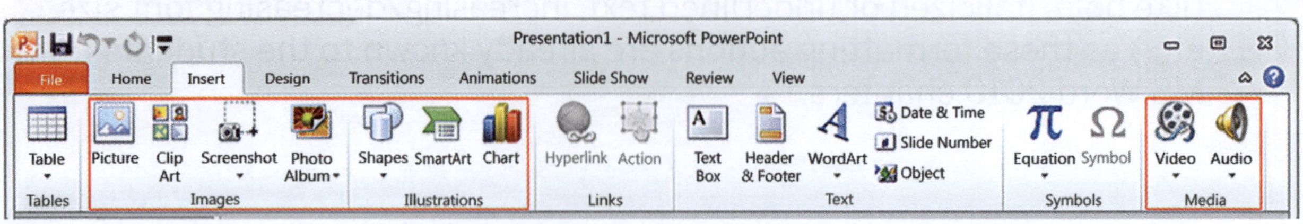

Fig. 7.1: Insert tab

INSERTING IMAGES AND ILLUSTRATIONS

The options to insert graphic elements like pictures, screenshots, shapes, charts, Clip Art or SmartArt are present in the **Images** and **Illustrations** group under the **Insert** tab. Let us see how we can use these objects to make our presentation attractive and creative.

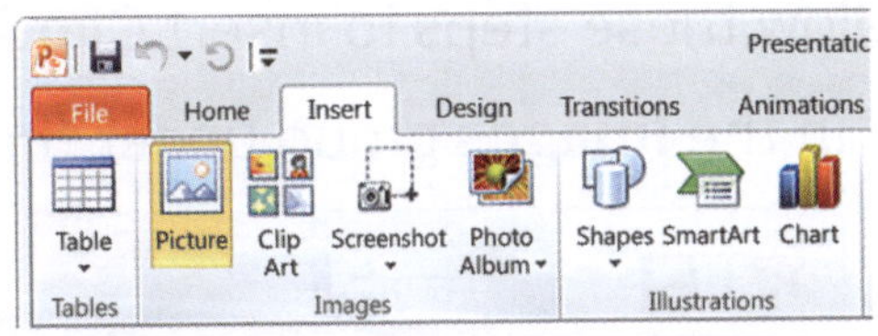

Fig. 7.2: Inserting a Picture

Inserting a Picture

To insert a picture in a presentation, follow the steps given below:

1. Click on the **Insert** tab.
2. In the **Images** group under the **Insert** tab, click on Picture (Fig. 7.2) to open the **Insert Picture** dialog box (Fig. 7.3).
3. Browse the folder which has the picture you want to insert. Select the picture and click on **Insert** to insert the picture.

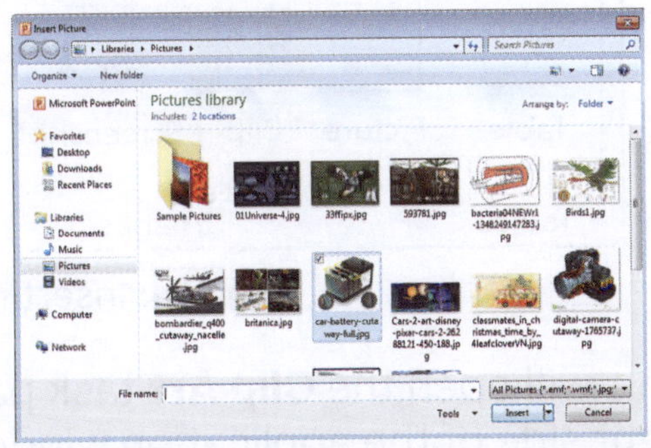

Fig. 7.3: Insert Picture dialog box

You Should Know

A screenshot is a way of taking a snapshot or a picture of your computer screen. MS PowerPoint 2010 allows you to capture a screenshot and add it to your presentation without having to leave MS PowerPoint. Click on **Screenshot** in the **Images** group under the **Insert** tab, to insert a screenshot.

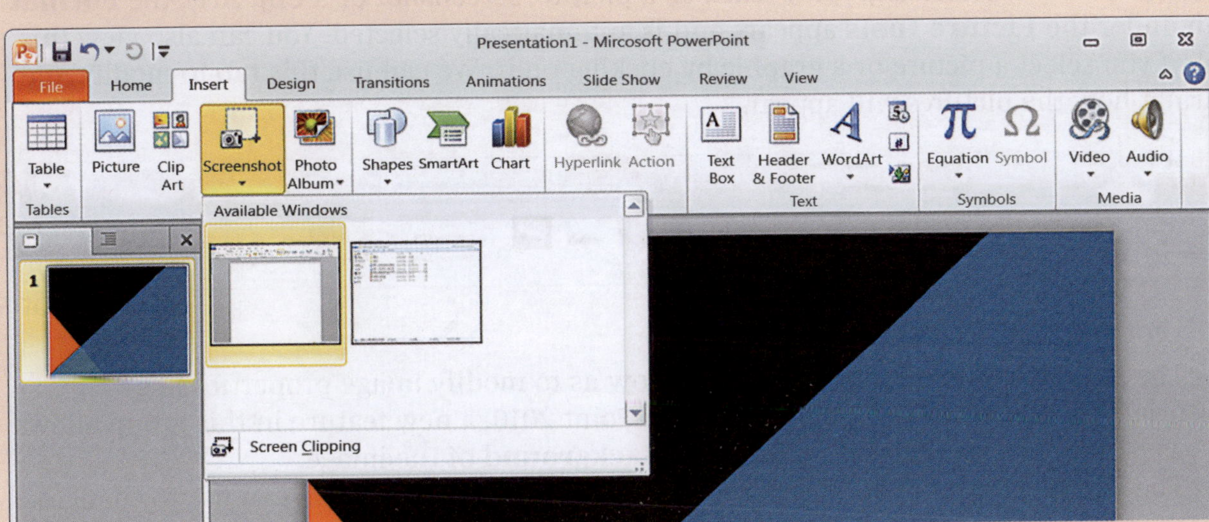

Inserting Clip Art

Clip Art is a collection of pictures or graphics, usually organized into categories, such as people, objects, nature, etc. that can be imported into a program. We can use Clip Art to make our PowerPoint presentations interesting.

Follow these steps to insert Clip Art in a slide:

1. In the **Images** group under the **Insert** tab, click on **Clip Art** (Fig. 7.4).

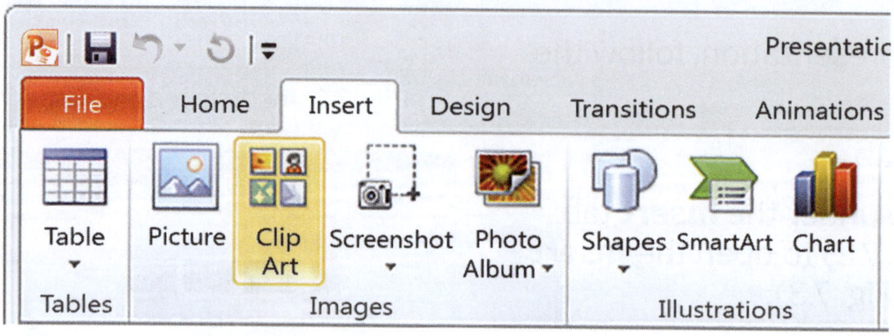

Fig. 7.4: Inserting a Clip Art

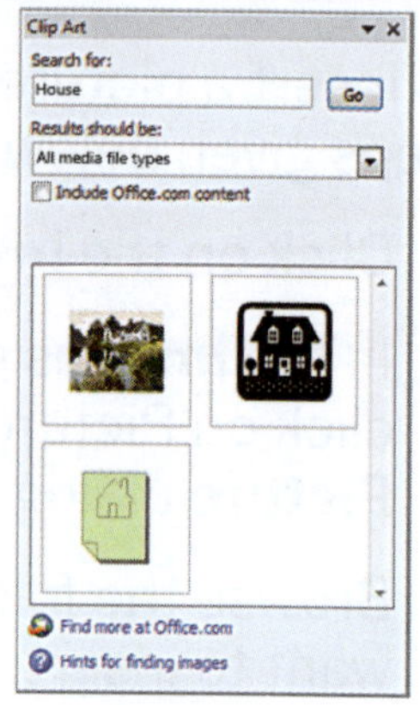

Fig. 7.5: Clip Art task pane

This will open the **Clip Art** task pane (Fig. 7.5) towards the right side of the application window.

2. Enter a suitable word or phrase in the **Search for** box and click on **Go** to view a set of pictures on the specified theme.
3. Select the Clip Art image you like and click on **Insert** to insert it in your slide.

You Should Know

After you have inserted a graphic (such as a picture, screenshot or a Clip Art), the **Format** tab under the **Picture Tools** appears and is automatically selected. You can also view this tab if you select a picture or a graphic by clicking on it. We can use this tab to modify and format how the pictures will appear.

The **Format** tab has four groups:

1. The **Adjust** group has options which allow us to modify image properties like brightness, contrast and colour. In PowerPoint 2010, a new feature in this group allows us to add **Artistic Effects** or **Remove Background** of the image.
2. The **Picture Styles** group has a set of predefined styles, which we can use to change the shape of the image, use borders and add other effects.

3. If there are two or more pictures in a slide, the **Arrange** group has options which allow us to organize the pictures—we can bring pictures to the front or send them behind other images.
4. The **Size** group gives us the options to resize or crop the images.

Also, the **Format** tab under **Picture Tools** is a contextual tab. These tabs are special tabs in the ribbon that are not visible all the time—they only appear when you are working on a particular slide object which can be edited using special options within these tabs.

Inserting a Shape

MS PowerPoint, like many other MS Office programs, has a collection of predefined shapes (Fig. 7.6).

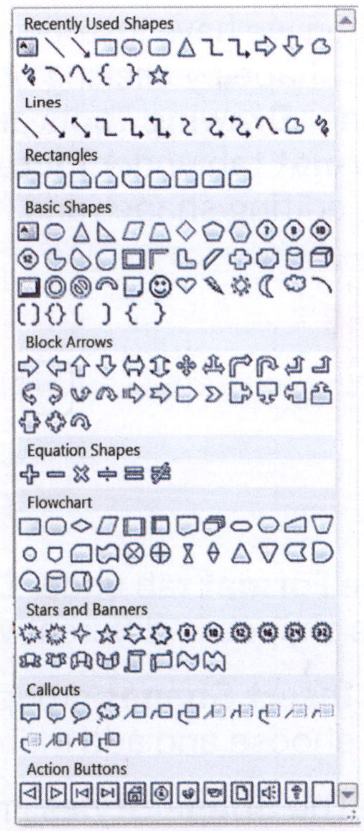

Fig. 7.6: Different sets of shapes

Let us see how we can use these shapes in our slides.

1. On the **Insert** tab in the **Illustrations** group, click **Shapes** (Fig. 7.7).

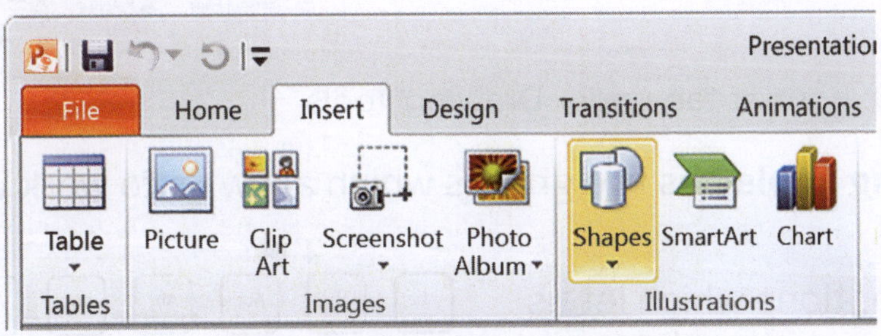

Fig. 7.7: Insert shapes

2. Click the shape that you want, click anywhere on the slide and then drag the mouse to place the shape.

You Should Know

To create a perfect square or circle while inserting a shape, press and hold the Shift key on your keyboard while you drag the mouse to draw the shape.

To resize or rotate a shape:

1. Click on the shape to select it.
2. Click and drag one of the sizing handles on the corners and sides of the text box until it is of the desired size (Fig. 7.8).

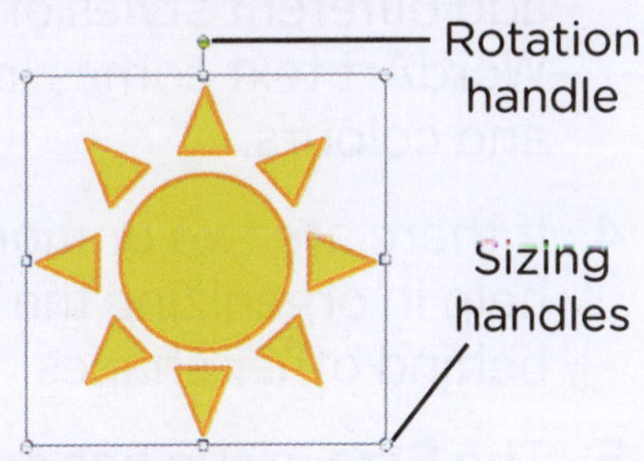

Fig. 7.8: Resizing a Shape

3. To rotate the shape, drag the green Rotation handle (Fig. 7.9).

Fig. 7.9: Rotating a shape

If you drag the sizing handles on any of the four corners, you will be able to change the height and width at the same time. The sizing handles on the top or bottom of the shape will only allow you to resize vertically, while the handles on the left and right sides will resize the shape horizontally.

Editing Shapes

When we have inserted a shape in a PowerPoint slide, or when we have selected the shape by clicking on it, the **Format** tab, which is a contextual tab, appears under **Drawing Tools** and is automatically selected (Fig. 7.10). This is similar to the **Format** tab under **Picture Tools**, but the **Format** tab under **Drawing Tools** is used for editing shapes and has the relevant options.

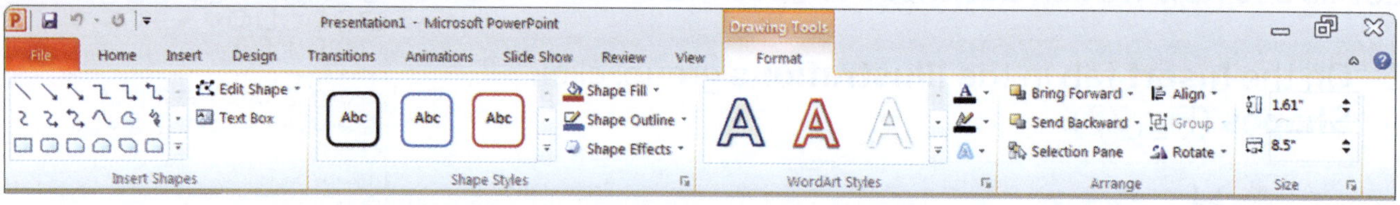

Fig. 7.10: Format tab under Drawing Tools

The **Format** tab under **Drawing Tools** has five groups which allow us to work with the shapes in different ways:

1. **Insert Shapes** group has options which let us choose and add more shapes to the slide.
2. The **Shape Styles** group controls the appearance of the shape—the fill colour, the outline colour, how the shape looks and other special options. Click the small arrow next to **Shape Styles** to open the **Shapes Style Gallery**, which shows us a number of styles to choose from (Fig. 7.11).
3. The **WordArt Styles** group allows you to add different styles of text to your shape. WordArt text comes in many different styles and colours.

Fig. 7.11: Shapes Styles Gallery

4. If there are two or more shapes in a slide, the **Arrange** group has options which help in organizing the shapes—we can bring shapes to the front or send them behind other shapes.
5. The **Size** group has options which allow us to resize the shape.

You Should Know

- To delete a shape from a slide, click the shape that you want to delete and then press the Delete key on your keyboard.
- To delete multiple shapes, press the Control key on your keyboard while you click the shapes that you want to delete and then press Delete.

Inserting SmartArt

MS PowerPoint includes a feature called SmartArt that allows you to add diagrams to your slides. SmartArt lets you create simple and effective diagrams, organization charts and flowcharts. **SmartArt** is usually divided into categories like List, Process, Cycle, Hierarchy, Relationship, Matrix, Pyramid and Picture and PowerPoint 2010 has more SmartArt templates than before.

To insert a SmartArt in your slide, follow these steps:

1. In the **Illustrations** group under the **Insert** tab, click on **SmartArt** (Fig. 7.12) to open the **Choose a SmartArt Graphic** dialog box (Fig. 7.13).

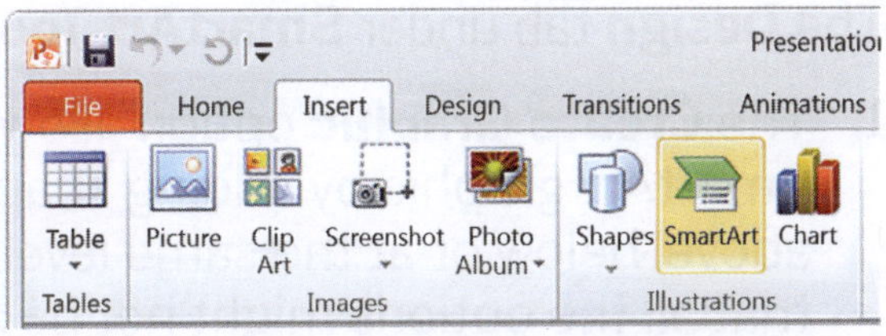

Fig. 7.12: Inserting a SmartArt

2. The SmartArt images are grouped as categories—you can view the options under a particular category or you can see all of them under the **All** option. Choose a SmartArt by clicking on the layout and click **OK** to insert it in your presentation.

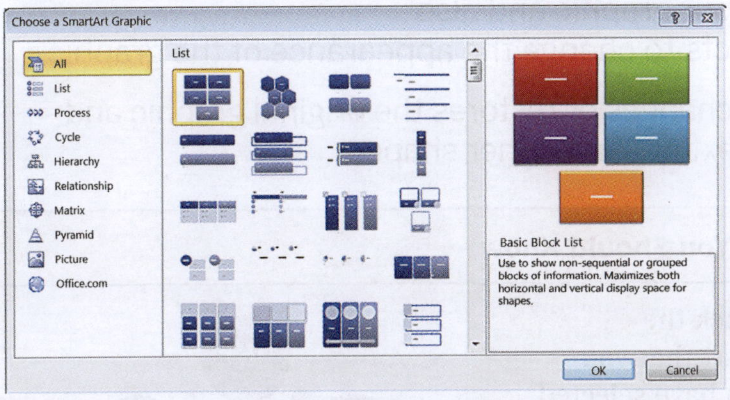

Fig. 7.13: Choose a SmartArt Graphic dialog box

3. After the SmartArt is inserted, you can click on each box with the option [Text] to enter the desired text. Fig. 7.14 shows a typical SmartArt (Radial Cycle SmartArt) from the **Cycle** group.

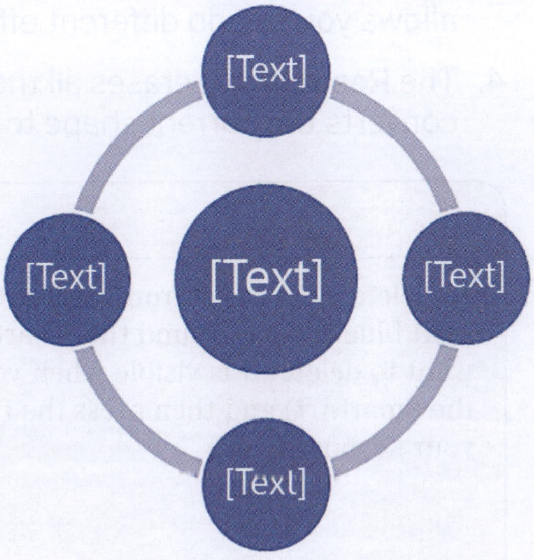

Fig. 7.14: Radial Cycle SmartArt

Editing SmartArt

Just after you have added a SmartArt or if you have a SmartArt graphic selected, two contextual tabs—**Format** tab and the **Design** tab appear under **SmartArt Tools** (Fig. 7.15).

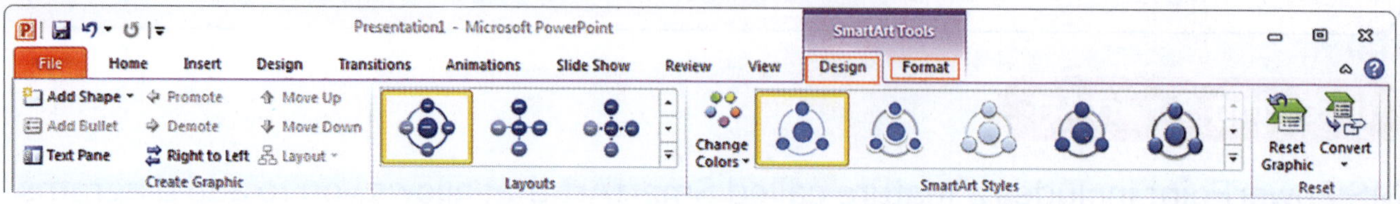

Fig. 7.15: Design and Format tabs

The **Format** tab under **SmartArt Tools** is almost the same as the **Format** tab under **Drawing Tools** or under **Picture Tools** and has similar options.

The **Design** tab under **SmartArt Tools** has four groups:

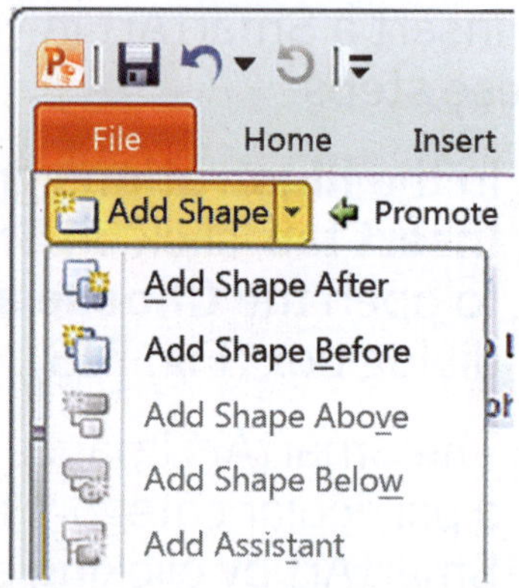

Fig. 7.16: Add Shape options

1. The **Create Graphic** option allows us to modify the SmartArt graphic by adding shapes after, before, above, below or at the same level (Fig. 7.16). Note that all the options might not be available for all SmartArt layouts.
2. The **Layouts** group allows us to replace the existing graphic with a different SmartArt.
3. The **SmartArt Styles** group lets you change the colour of the selected part of your graphic and also allows you to add different effects to change the appearance of the graphic.
4. The **Reset** group erases all the changes or restores the original graphic and converts the current shape to text or some other shape.

You Should Know

To delete a SmartArt from a slide, click the light blue border around the SmartArt that you want to delete (it is visible when you have selected the SmartArt) and then press the Delete key on your keyboard.

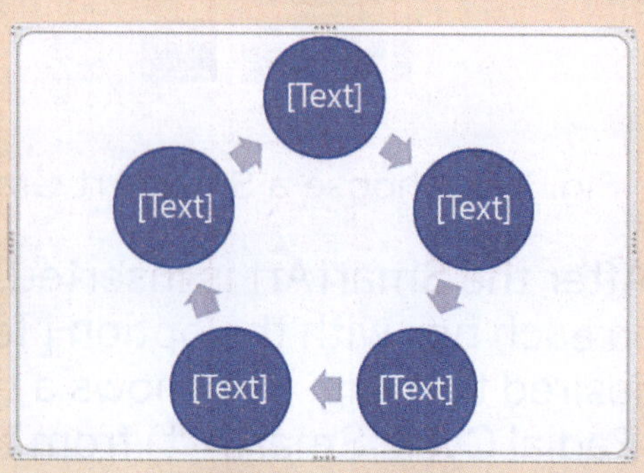

Creating a Photo Album

If you would like to create a slide show just using pictures or have a section of your presentation with just pictures, you can use the **Photo Album** tool in PowerPoint.

1. Click **Photo Album** in the **Images** group under the **Insert** tab and choose **New Photo Album** (Fig. 7.17).

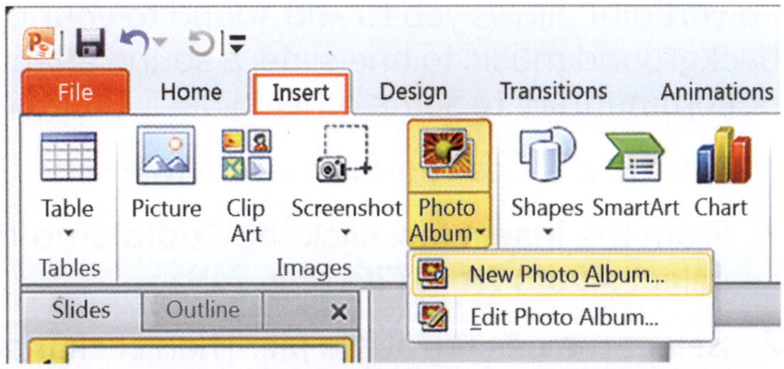

Fig. 7.17: Creating a Photo Album

2. The **Photo Album** dialog box opens (Fig. 7.18). Below **Insert picture from**, click on the **File/Disk...** button to choose your images from your hard disk. Select your images (use the **Shift** key or **Control** key to select multiple images). Once you have selected the images, you can see the names of the images in the **Pictures in album** box. To preview a particular image, click on it. Note that the list in the **Pictures in album** box is alphabetical–you can change the order by using the up and down arrows at bottom of that list.

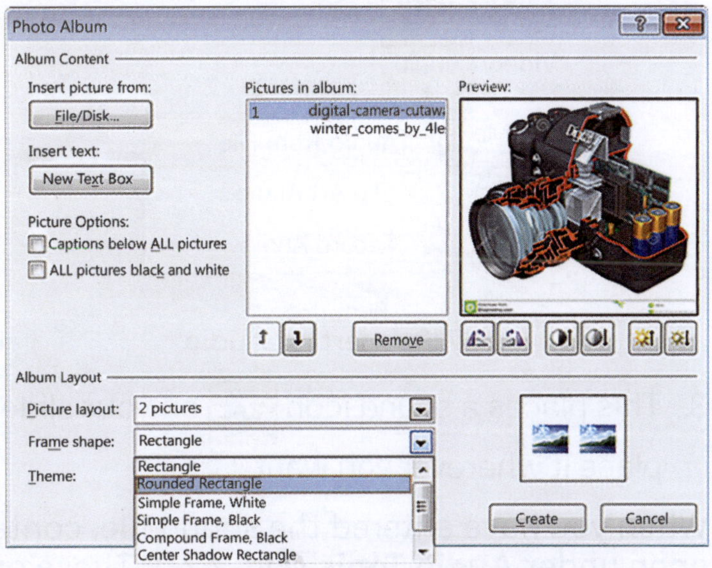

Fig. 7.18: Photo Album dialog box

3. In the **Album Layout** section, choose how many images you would like per slide in the **Picture layout** box. Choose a frame for your photos if you want one using the **Frame shape** box. Click on the **Create** button and the slides will be created.

You Should Know

- If you choose the Photo Album option while in a presentation, a new presentation is created with the new slides. You can then copy and paste them into your original presentation.
- You can also edit the photo album you have created at any time by clicking on the **Photo Album** in the ribbon and choosing **Edit Photo Album**.

INSERTING AN AUDIO

PowerPoint allows you to add sound to your presentation . You may want to add background music to one slide, a sound effect to another or maybe add narration or commentary to some other slides.

Follow these steps to add an audio to a slide:

1. From the **Insert** tab, click the **Audio** drop-down arrow in the **Media** group and select **Audio from File** (Fig. 7.19).
2. Select the desired audio file. Then click **Insert** (Fig. 7.20).

Fig. 7.19: Inserting Audio

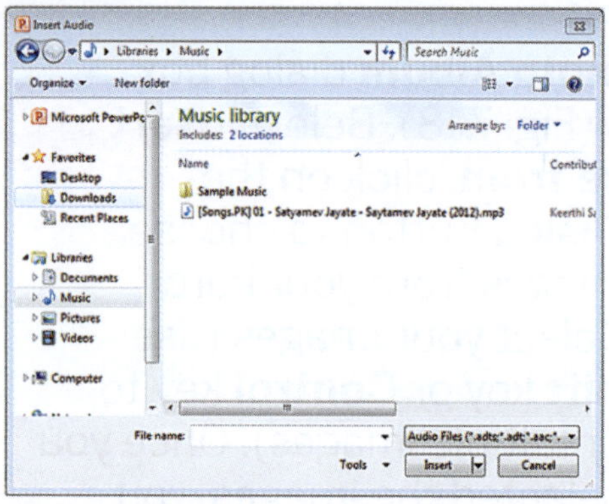

Fig. 7.20: Insert Audio dialog box

3. This places a sound icon  on your slide. You can drag the sound icon and place it wherever you want.

When you have entered the sound file, contextual tabs Format and Playback open under **Audio Tools** (Fig. 7.21). These options can be used to modify the audio file.

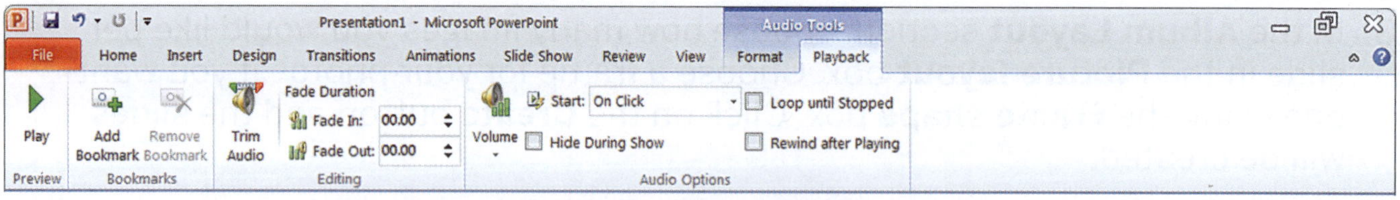

Fig. 7.21: Options tab

> **You Should Know**
>
> You can also insert sound clips using **Clip Art Audio** option or use **Record Audio** to record and insert an audio file.

INSERTING A VIDEO

You can also add videos to your presentation. Follow the steps given below to add a video to a slide:

1. From the **Insert** tab, click the **Video** drop-down arrow in the **Media** group and select **Video from File** (Fig. 7.22). Note that you can also use a Clip Art video or a video from a website.
2. The **Insert Video** dialog box appears. Navigate to the folder containing the video file and click to select it. Click **Insert** to insert the video clip.

Fig. 7.22: Inserting video

3. Click on the video clip area and use the resize handles to resize it, if necessary. It will play within the presentation if you click on it.

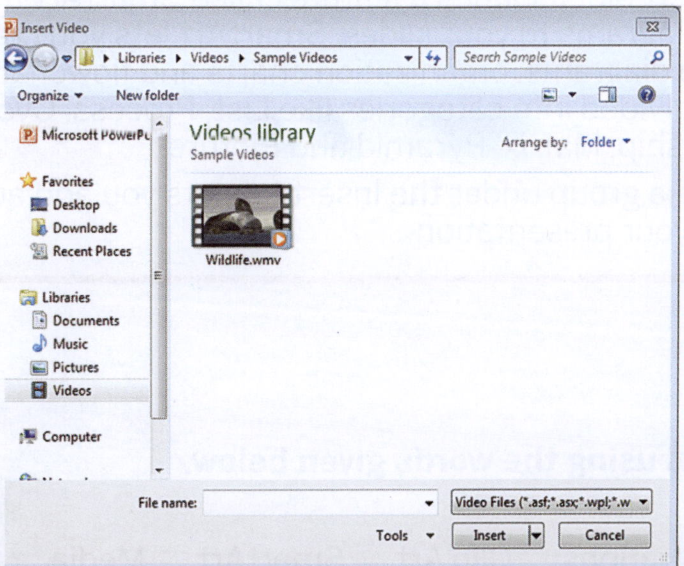

Fig. 7.23: Insert Video dialog box

When you have inserted the video file, contextual tabs **Format** and **Playback** open under **Video Tools** (Fig. 7.24). These options can be used to enhance and add effects to the video file selected.

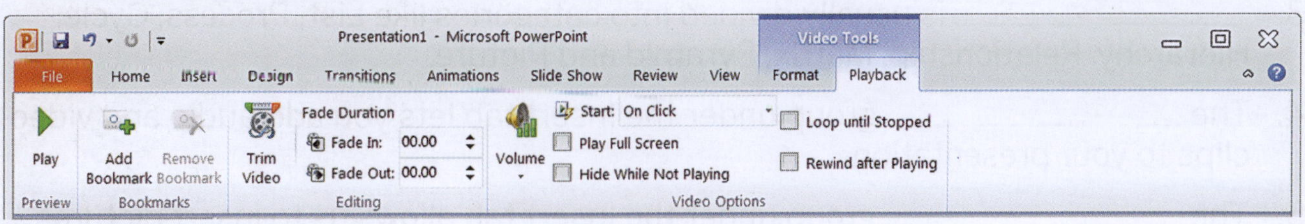

Fig. 7.24: Video tools

Quick Recap

1. The Insert tab in MS PowerPoint has the options for adding various objects to enhance a presentation.
2. A screenshot is a way of taking a snapshot or a picture of your computer screen.
3. Clip Art is a collection of pictures or graphics, organized into categories such as people, objects, nature, etc. that can be imported into a program.
4. The Images and Illustrations group under the Insert tab allows us to insert pictures, shapes, screenshots, photo albums, Clip Art and SmartArt.
5. Contextual tabs are special tabs in the ribbon that are not visible all the time. They appear when you are working with a particular slide object which can be edited using special options within these tabs.
6. MS PowerPoint includes a feature called SmartArt that allows you to add diagrams to your slides. SmartArt lets you create simple and effective diagrams, organization charts and flowcharts. SmartArt is usually divided into categories like List, Process, Cycle, Hierarchy, Relationship, Matrix, Pyramid and Picture.
7. The Media group under the Insert tab lets you add audio or video clips to your presentation.

EXERCISE

A Fill in the blanks using the words given below.

Images and Illustrations   Clip Art   SmartArt   Media   Contextual tabs

1. ________________ are special tabs in the ribbon that are not visible all the time.
2. ________________________ is a collection of pictures or graphics, organized into categories such as people, objects, nature, etc, that can be imported into a program.
3. ________________ is usually divided into categories like List, Process, Cycle, Hierarchy, Relationship, Matrix, Pyramid and Picture.
4. The ________________ group under the Insert tab lets you add audio and video clips to your presentation.
5. The ________________ group under the Insert tab allows us to insert pictures, shapes, screenshots, Clip Art and SmartArt.

B Write the steps involved in the following.

1. Adding a picture to a slide
2. Creating a photo album in MS PowerPoint
3. Adding an audio to a slide

C Answer the following questions briefly.

1. What are contextual tabs? Give examples.
2. What are screenshots?
3. How can you delete a SmartArt from a slide?

Lab Activity FA

Make a PowerPoint presentation on your school. Include photographs of different sections of your school in the presentation to describe your school. Ask your teacher to help you if you do not find pictures of different classes of the school. Write the steps you have followed while inserting pictures.

Research Project FA

Use the SmartArt feature in MS PowerPoint to prepare a presentation on water cycle. The adjacent image has been given as a clue.

Teacher's Notes

Explain how contextual tabs appear depending on which objects are selected in the presentation.

Demonstrate and explain the different options available on the Insert tab and how to edit pictures/SmartArt.

8 Internet for Connecting with People

Learning Objectives

By the end of this chapter you should be able to
- learn about Social Networking.
- know about Online Gaming.
- understand Online Telephony.
- perform Online File Sharing.

Introduction

Internet, an important and fundamental mode of modern-day communication, is a vast computer network which connects millions of computers all over the world with one another and makes information sharing between these machines possible.

We have already learnt how we can use the Internet to browse web pages, search for information using popular search engines like Google, and send and receive emails using email service providers like Gmail, Yahoo and Hotmail.

Internet offers many methods of connecting with people—chatting, blogs, instant messaging and social networking websites. Internet users can play games over the Internet with one another, share files online and use a variety of other services like e-greetings, e-cards and Internet telephony. Let us study some of the services the Internet offers.

SOCIAL NETWORKING

A social networking service allows people, who share interests or real-life connections, to build social networks or social relations. A social network service consists of a representation of each user's information (usually called a profile), his social links and a variety of additional services. When it comes to online social networking, websites are commonly used. These websites are known as social networking websites which serve as an online community of Internet users. Figures 8.1 and 8.2 are the social networking sites, sixdegrees and friendster.

Fig. 8.1: Sixdegrees interface

As early as in 1978, two Chicago computer hobbyists invented the bulletin board system (BBS) to inform friends about the meetings, make announcements and share information through postings. This was one of the first attempts to share information using the Internet.

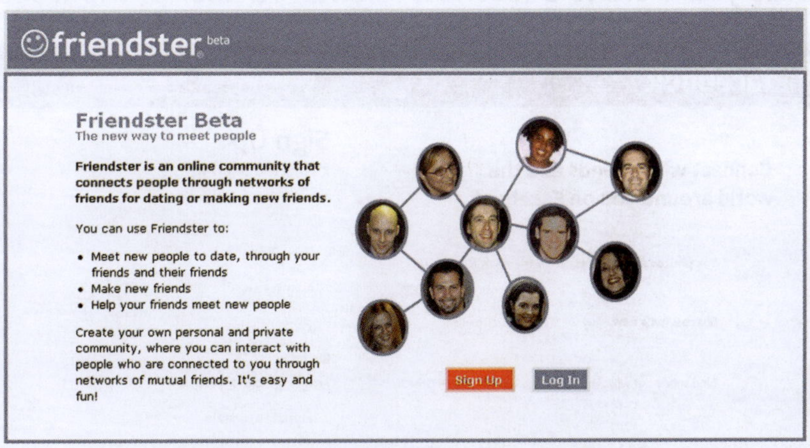

Fig. 8.2: Friendster interface

By 1997, social networking sites like sixdegrees, which allowed users to create profiles and list friends, became popular. Friendster, a social networking website, was launched in 2002 and grew to 3 million users in three months. 2003 saw the coming of Myspace. Facebook was launched in 2004 and Twitter in 2006.

Let us take a look at some of the most popular social networking websites.

Myspace

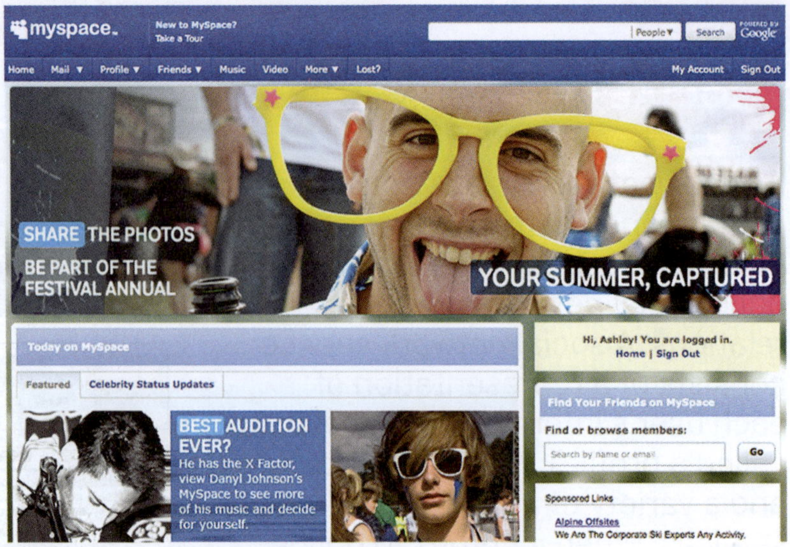

Fig. 8.3: Myspace interface

Myspace was founded in 2003 by Chris DeWolfe and Tom Anderson. It allows a user to create a profile that can be shared with friends and family. Myspace has a significant focus on music and music sharing.

From 2005 until early 2008, Myspace was the most-visited social networking site in the world and in June 2006 it surpassed Google as the most-visited website in the United States. However, the website indulged in heavy advertising which made the website sluggish and less easy to use. By April 2008, Facebook had more worldwide users than Myspace.

Facebook

Facebook was founded on 4 February 2004 by Mark Zuckerberg while he was a student at Harvard University, USA. Initially, only Harvard University students could become Facebook members. Later, it extended its services to various other universities before it opened to a worldwide public. Facebook now allows anyone who is more than 13 years old to become a registered user of the website.

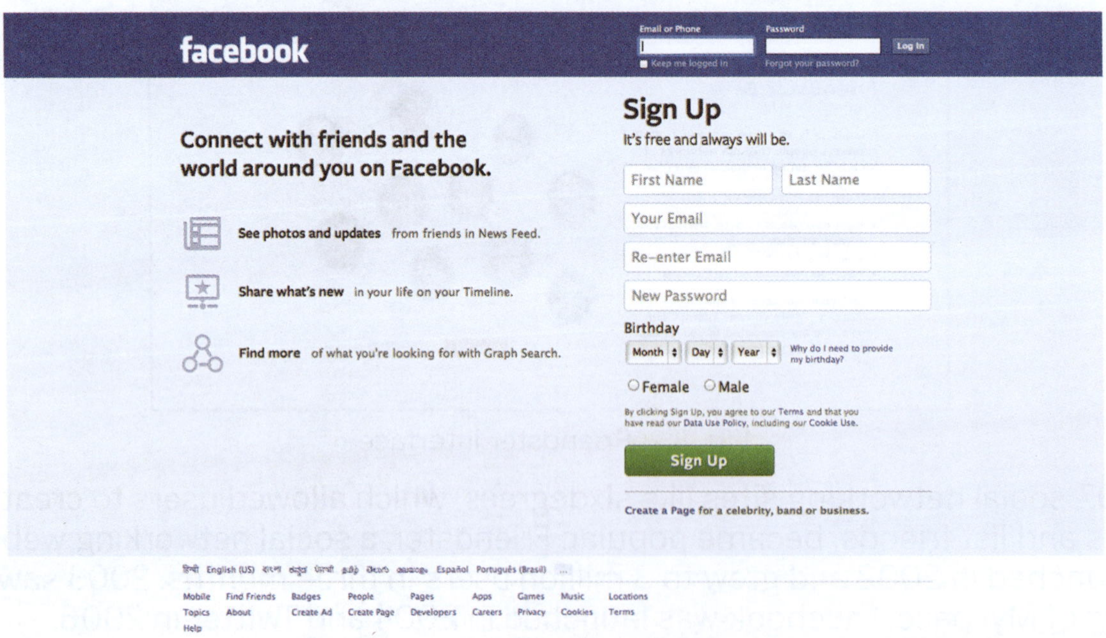

Fig. 8.4: Facebook interface

Users need to register before using the website. A registered user may create a personal profile, add other users as friends, exchange messages and receive automatic notifications. Additionally, users may join common-interest groups and categorize their friends into lists.

Facebook is the most popular social networking website with over one billion active users.

Apart from individual users, many companies, institutions and organizations also have Facebook pages and accounts.

Twitter

Twitter is an online social networking service that allows its users to send and read short text messages of maximum 140 characters which are called *tweets*. Registered users can read and post tweets, but unregistered users can only read tweets posted by others.

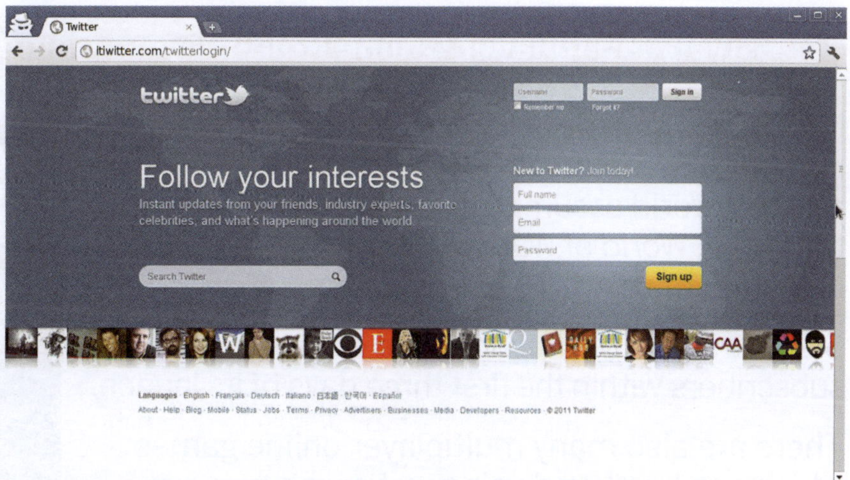

Fig. 8.5: Twitter interface

Twitter was created in 2006 by Jack Dorsey and rapidly gained worldwide popularity. Twitter is now one of the 10 most-visited websites and has been described as 'the SMS of the Internet'.

Many famous people and organizations have Twitter accounts—Barack Obama, the US President, has one of the most popular Twitter accounts with more than 40 million people following his tweets.

You Should Know

Most social networking sites like Facebook, Twitter and Myspace have dedicated apps for smartphones and other hand-held devices.

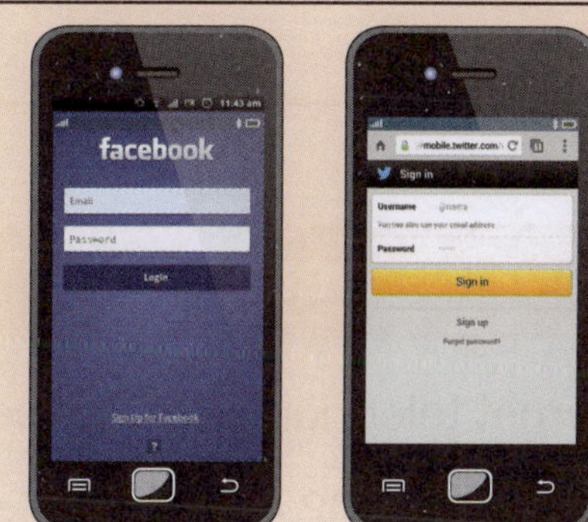

ONLINE GAMING

An online game is a computer game played over the Internet or a computer network. As computer networks grew from small local networks to the Internet and as Internet became accessible to more users, it allowed the growth of online gaming also. Modern-day online games can use complex graphics and virtual worlds populated by many players at the same time. Many online games have an associated online community where members can discuss issues related to the game, making online games a form of social activity.

Massively Multiplayer Online Role-playing Games (MMORPGs)

MMORPGs are special online games where a large number of people from all over the world can join a virtual world assuming the role of a character in the game. *World of Warcraft*, a popular MMORPG, has more than 7 million subscribers.

Star Wars: The Old Republic had one million subscribers within the first three days of its launch.

There are also many multiplayer online games which can be played using just a web browser. Browser games like *Farmville* and *Travian* are very popular among users.

Fig. 8.6: World of Warcraft

You Should Know

Smartphones and other hand-held devices have helped in the development of online gaming immensely.

More and more users can stay online using mobile technology and mobile game apps allow users to join an online game from any location.

ONLINE TELEPHONY

Internet telephony enables people to use the Internet as a medium for telephone calls.

If you are using a computer which is connected to the Internent, you can use an Internet telephony software to call any other computer using the same software or you can call on any phone number anywhere in the world. International telephone calls are much less expensive using Internet telephony.

One of the most popular Internet telephony software is Skype which can be downloaded from *www.skype.com*.

To use Internet telephony, you need the following:

(a) a computer connected to the Internet

(b) a microphone

(c) an Internet telephony software

(d) a speaker or a headphone

ONLINE FILE SHARING

An online file-sharing service provides a way to store and access information such as documents, data, photos and videos, using the Internet rather than storing the information locally on a hard drive. The term *cloud* is used to denote the online virtual space where the information is stored. Hence, this method of storing information is also sometimes called the *cloud storage*.

Fig. 8.7: OneDrive

There are a number of online file-sharing services like Microsoft OneDrive, Dropbox, Google Drive, Picasa, Flickr and YouTube. Most of these can be accessed using a PC or a smartphone, provided the user has access rights.

Fig. 8.8: Google Drive

Cloud-based file sharing services allow users to create special folders on their computers or mobile devices. These folders are then synchronized online, so that the folder can be viewed by different users from other computers. This folder can usually be accessed through a website or a mobile app. Dropbox and Google Drive are two such popular file-sharing services.

Many file-sharing services are dedicated to hosting particular types of data—for example, Picasa for photographs and other images and Youtube for videos.

Picasa

Picasa is a free image organizer and image viewer for organizing and editing digital photos. It has an integrated website for sharing photos. Picasa was originally created in 2002 by a company named Lifescape. It is owned by Google since 2004. The latest version of Picasa is 3.9 (released in the year 2014).

Picasa allows us to share our photos online with our friends as well as maintain a backup of our images.

To use Picasa:

1. The user has to download the Picasa program from *http://picasa.google.co.in/* and install it.
2. When this program is opened, it automatically finds all the pictures stored in the computer and displays them. The user can then upload the chosen photos to an online Picasa Web Album by clicking on **Upload** (Fig. 8.9).

Fig. 8.9: Uploading photos on Picasa

You Should Know

When photos taken with a smartphone are uploaded, Picasa can use the **Geotagging** feature to automatically set the location for the photos, using the phone's location settings. **Face recognition** is another modern feature in Picasa which allows the software to automatically detect and tag faces.

YouTube

YouTube is an online video-sharing website created in February 2005 and owned by Google since 2006. Users can upload, view and share videos on YouTube. The link to access YouTube is *www.youtube.com*.

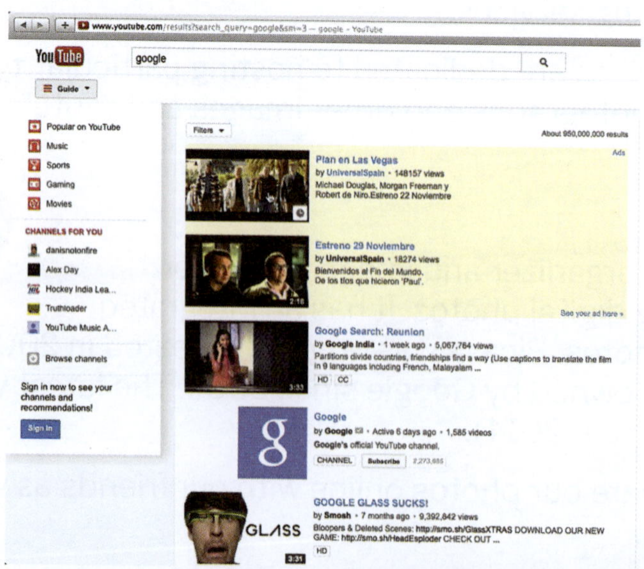

Fig. 8.10: YouTube interface

You Should Know

The first YouTube video was titled *Me at the Zoo* and shows its cofounder Jawed Karim at a zoo. The video was uploaded in 2005 and can still be viewed on the website.

BLOGS

The word blog originally came from the word *weblog* or a *web log*. A blog usually is a website which has posts (or entries). The most recent entries usually appear first and the oldest entries appear last. A user can use a blog to write about any particular area of interest or on any topic that fascinates him. A blog is updated frequently and regularly. This makes a blog somewhat like a journal or a diary.

The person who writes a blog is called a *blogger*, and the act of writing, posting or maintaining a blog is called *blogging*. Blogs can have individual authors or a collection of authors.

Two very popular blogging websites are www.*wordpress.com and www.blogger.com.*

E-GREETINGS

There are several websites through which we can send e-greeting cards specially designed for a happy or a festive occasion.

Some popular websites which have a good collection of e-greetings are:

- *www.bharathgreetings.com*
- *www.123greetings.com*
- *www.someecards.com*

We can use these websites to send e-greeting cards to our friends and family on different occasions like birthdays, Christmas, Holi, Eid and Diwali. Some of these websites even allow us to schedule a card before the event, so that the website would send the card to the recipient on the date of the festival or the event.

You can send an e-greetings card to one person or to a group of people.

Quick Recap

1. Internet is a vast computer network which connects millions of computers all over the world with each other and makes information sharing between these machines possible.
2. A social networking service allows people, who share interests or real-life connections, to build social networks or social relations.
3. Myspace was founded in 2003 by Chris DeWolfe and Tom Anderson. It allows a user to create a profile that can be shared with friends and family. Myspace focusses on music and music sharing.
4. Facebook, a very popular social networking website, was founded on 4 February 2004 by Mark Zuckerberg.
5. Twitter is an online social networking service that allows its users to send and read short messages which are called tweets.
6. An online game is a computer game played over the Internet or a computer network.
7. Massively Multiplayer Online Role-playing Games (MMORPGs) are special online games where a large number of people from all over the world can join a virtual world assuming the role of a character in the game.
8. There are many multiplayer online games which can be played using just the web browser. Browser games like Farmville and Travian are very popular among users.
9. Internet telephony enables people to use the Internet as a medium for telephone calls. One of the most popular Internet telephony software is Skype.
10. An online file-sharing service provides a way to store and access information such as documents, data, photos and video, using the Internet rather than storing the information locally on a hard drive.
11. The term cloud is used to denote the online virtual space where the information is stored. Hence, this method of storing information is also sometimes called cloud storage.
12. Picasa is a free image organizer and image viewer for organizing and editing digital photos.
13. YouTube is an online video-sharing website created in February 2005 and owned by Google since 2006.
14. Blog originally came from the word weblog or a web log. A blog is a website which has posts. The most recent entries usually appear first and the oldest entries appear last.
15. There are several websites through which we can send an e-greeting card specially designed for the special occasion and festivals.

EXERCISE

A Fill in the blanks using the words given below.

Google Drive   YouTube   Twitter   Facebook   Picasa

1. ________________ was founded on 4 February 2004 by Mark Zuckerberg.
2. ________________ is an online social networking service that allows its users to send and read short text messages of maximum 140 characters.
3. ________________ is a free image organizer and image viewer for organizing and editing digital photos.
4. ________________ is an online video-sharing website created in February 2005 and owned by Google since 2006.
5. ________________ is an example of a file-sharing service.

B Match the following.

Column A	Column B
(a) Blog	(i) allows people to build social networks or social relations
(b) Cloud	(ii) provides a way to store and access information such as documents, data, photos and video, using the Internet
(c) Online file-sharing service	(iii) the online virtual space where the information is stored
(d) Online game	(iv) originally comes from the word weblog
(e) Social networking service	(v) a computer game played over the Internet or a computer network

C Answer the following questions.

1. What is Internet telephony? Give an example.
2. What is a social networking website? Give examples of three such websites.
3. What is an MMORPG? Give an example of an MMORPG.
4. What is a blog?

Lab Activity

FA

Search names of five social networking websites on the Internet. Write their names in your notebook. Now, search names of two MMORPGs on the Internet. Write their names in your notebook.

Now, compare the names you have written with your friends. Are there any names which are common?

For finding this information on the Internet, make sure the computer in the lab is connected to the Internet (ask your teacher to help you if it is not connected).

Research Project

FA

Vivek has collected about 20 pictures of his school and wants to share these pictures with his friends. Which program should he use for doing this?

Help him by telling him how to do this?

Also, find a list of similar programs which help to share the pictures and videos.

Teacher's Notes

The teacher must discuss about online safety and netiquette. The students should be made aware of the online privacy issues and the dangers of befriending strangers, especially when using social networking sites.

Also, demonstrate the use of Picasa and some other websites (Google Drive, Dropbox, 123egreetings.com, etc.) encouraging students to navigate the websites themselves.

WORKSHEET

A Unscramble the words and fill in the blanks.

1. ________________ is a spreadsheet program from the MS Office suite of programs. (EELSMXC)
2. To start MS Excel, open the Run dialog box and type ________________ and then press Enter. (EELCX)
3. The ________________ at the bottom left side of the Excel window indicates the worksheets present in the workbook. (THESE BAT)
4. The rows and columns intersect to form ________________. (SCLLE)
5. The ________________ displays the cell reference or the address of the active cell. (ENMA XBO)

B Write the steps to perform the following actions.

1. Saving a workbook in MS Excel
2. Adding SmartArt to a slide in PowerPoint
3. Opening a new workbook in MS Excel
4. Adding audio to a slide in PowerPoint
5. Uploading a set of photos to Picasa
6. Creating a photo album in PowerPoint

C Give one word for each of the following.

1. The smallest unit of an MS Excel worksheet.
2. The tab that shows which worksheet is currently active.
3. The last column name.
4. Special tabs in the ribbon that are not visible all the time but appear only when you are working with a particular slide object which can be edited using special options on these tabs.
5. The keyboard button we have to press to create a perfect square or circle while we drag the mouse to draw the shape.
6. A social networking site founded in 2003 by Chris DeWolfe and Tom Anderson.
7. A social networking site founded in 2004 by Mark Zuckerberg.
8. Example of a contextual tab in MS PowerPoint 2010.

D Answer the following questions briefly.

1. What is a formula bar in MS Excel? Where is it located?
2. How can you insert a video in a PowerPoint presentation?
3. What is online gaming? Give some examples of online games.
4. What is Internet telephony? Name one of the most popular Internet telephony software.
5. What is YouTube?
6. What are blogs? Who is a blogger?
7. What are e-greetings? How are e-greeting cards useful? Name two popular e-greeting websites.

Projects

Start MS Excel 2010. Open a new workbook.

Enter the names of all the states in India under column A and the names of their capitals under Column B. Use the Internet to help you search and find all the names of the states and their capitals. The screen shows the names of a few states with their capitals.

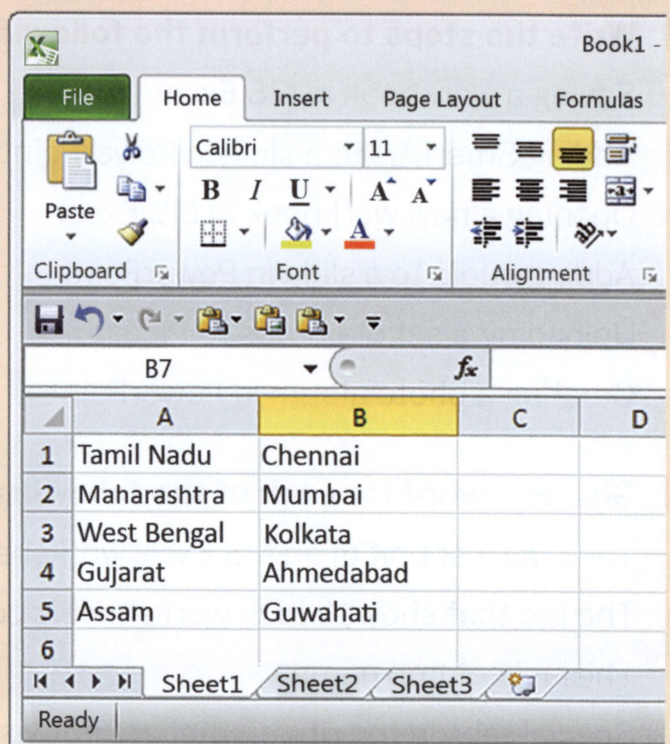

When you have entered all the states and their capitals, save the workbook as *Capitals of India.*

What was the extension with which the file name was saved?

Close Excel.

Write the steps you have followed to open and close the Excel sheet and to create and save the workbook.

ASSESSMENT 1

Chapters 1-3

(Maximum Marks: 20)

A Complete the following table. **(5 × 1 = 5)**

________________ PB = 1024 TB
1 ________________ = 1024 MB
1 TB = ________________ GB
1 MB = 1024 ________________
1 KB = ________________ bytes

B Fill in the blanks. **(5)**

1. In computers, binary digits are usually grouped together into collections of eight, called ____________.
2. A computer, like many other electronic machines, uses only two digits ____________ and ____________ to represent all information.
3. A ____________ is the smallest unit of data a computer can handle.
4. While measuring storage capacity, the letters GB stand for ____________.

C Answer the following questions briefly. **(10)**

1. What is an MSWLogo procedure? Give an example. **(2)**
2. What are the rules for naming an MSWLogo procedure? **(2)**
3. What will be the output of the following MSWLogo command:
   REPEAT 40 [REPEAT 360 [FD1 RT1] RT10] **(2)**
4. Write the commands to get the MSWLogo procedure called SHAPE to draw the figure you got as the output for the above question. **(4)**

ASSESSMENT 2

Chapters 4-5

(Maximum Marks: 20)

A The following is a list of five students in a class and the marks they got in English and Maths: **(15)**

Name of Student	Marks in English	Marks in Maths
Yusuf	86	92
Sameer	81	99
Gurvinder	89	91
Meera	87	93
Shelly	82	98

Help the teacher compose a letter informing each student his or her marks using the Mail Merge feature in MS Word.

(Hint: It may help if you create customized columns called *Name, Marks in English* and *Marks in Maths* in the Customize Address List dialog box.)

The following is one of the letters given as a clue. Use it to create the main document. You should use your teacher's name instead of the given sender's name.

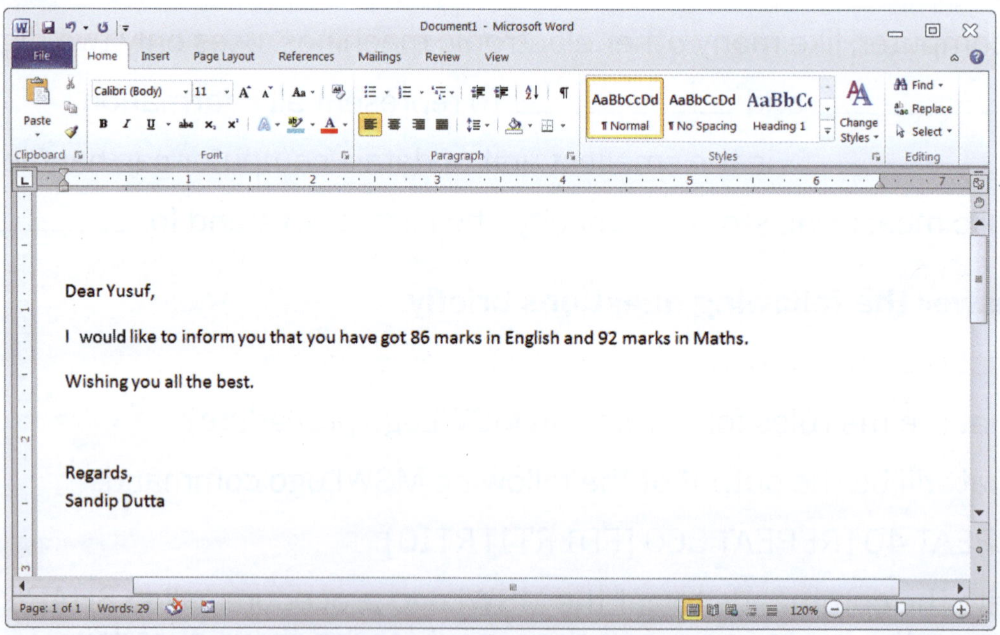

B Shyamal needs to explain how to add a footnote to an MS Word 2010 document. Write the steps that he would follow. **(5)**

ASSESSMENT 3

Chapters 6-8

(Maximum Marks: 20)

A Make a presentation with four slides giving details about each of the following: **(4 × 2 = 8)**

1. Blu-ray disc
2. CD
3. DVD
4. Floppy disk

B Write a line about each of the following. **(4 × 1 = 4)**

1. Social networking
2. Online gaming
3. Online telephony
4. Online file sharing

C What is the difference between: **(4 × 1 = 4)**

1. Active Cell and Active Sheet
2. Name Box and Formula Bar
3. Status Bar and View Bar
4. Vertical Scroll Bar and Horizontal Scroll Bar

D Identify the following logos. **(4 × 1 = 4)**

1.
2. Google Drive
3. Picasa
4. 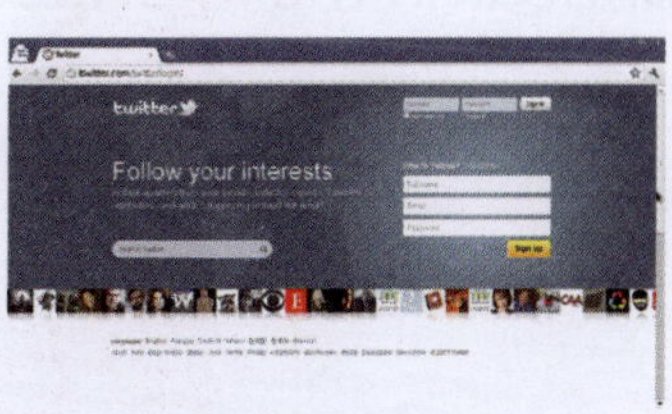

REVISION QUESTIONS

Suggested Questions for SA

(Maximum Marks: 50)

A Unscramble the words given at the end of each sentence and fill in the blanks. (5 × 1 = 5)

1. ______________ memory is generally made up of semiconductor devices, while ______________ memory devices are usually magnetic or optical. (PYRAIRM/YSCENORAD)
2. A ______________ is a graphical or symbolic representation of the sequential instructions necessary to perform a task. (RALFOHCWT)
3. A procedure contains the sequential list of ______________ that the procedure will execute. (MCADNOMS)
4. We can see all the procedures that are currently defined in MSWLogo by clicking on the ______________ button in the ______________ window. (LLADE/MMREDCANO)
5. Commands for inserting and editing footnotes and endnotes can be found on the ______________ tab in the ______________ group. (RREEEEFCSN/OOOTTFESN)

B Answer the following questions briefly. (10 × 2 = 20)

1. How can we use the current system date as a header in MS Word 2010?
2. What is a data source in a Mail Merge document?
3. What is the Name Box in MS Excel?
4. Describe any one method of saving a workbook in MS Excel. What is the extension of an Excel 2010 file?
5. What is Clip Art? How can you insert Clip Art into a PowerPoint slide?
6. What is an online file-sharing service? Why do we use it?
7. Give two examples of online file-sharing services.
8. Name some devices which have inbuilt memory.
9. How is algorithm different from a flowchart?
10. What is a separator line in MS Word? When does it appear in the interface?

C The screen shown below has the following components: **(10 × 2 = 20)**

1. File Tab
2. Sheet Tab
3. Active Sheet
4. Row Numbers
5. Column Names
6. Active Cell
7. Name Box
8. Formula Bar
9. Quick Access Toolbar
10. Ribbon

Label each component on the screen and write what is the name of the software to which this application window belongs. Also, write a line about each component.

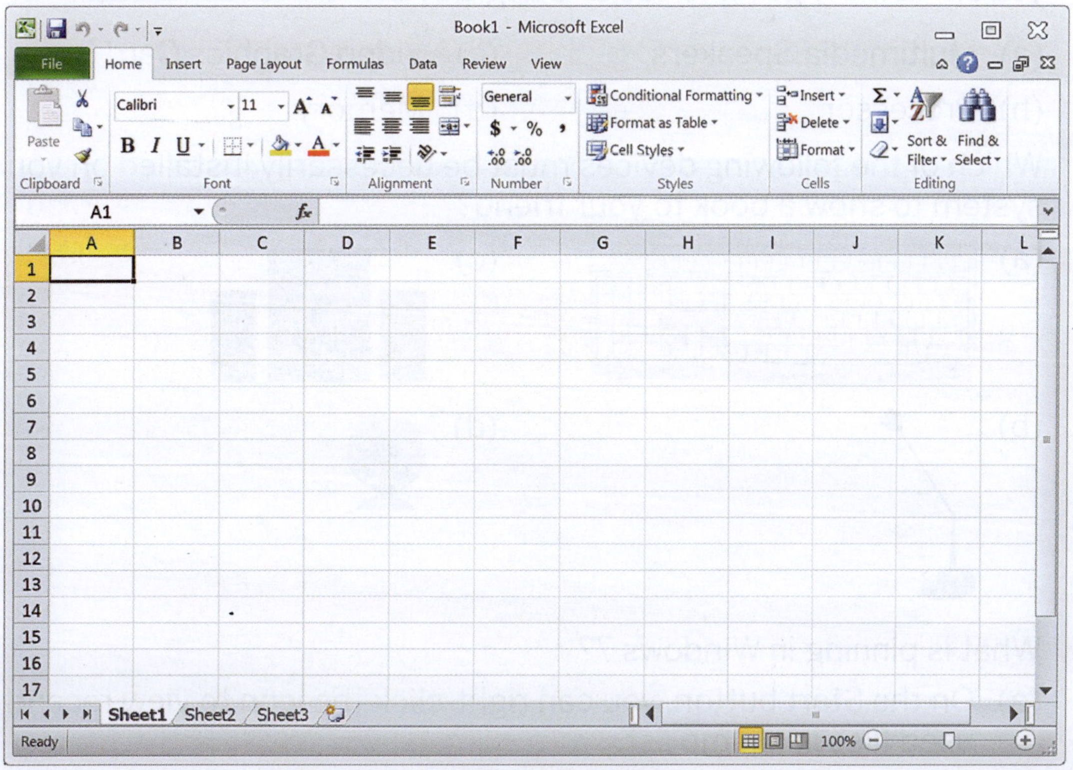

D Write two features of each of the following. **(5 × 1 = 5)**

1. ROM
2. Connectors
3. Procedure
4. SmartArt
5. Merge fields

1. Find the odd one out.

(a) 

(c) 

(b) 

(d) 

2. You have been suggested to upgrade the GPU on your desktop computer, you are actually going to add and upgrade ________________ .

(a) Multimedia Speakers
(c) Video Graphics Card
(b) Processor
(d) Memory

3. Which of the following devices must be necessarily installed on your system to show a book to your friend?

(a) 

(c) 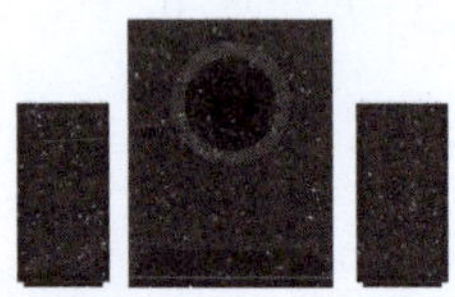

(b) 

(d) 

4. What is pinning in Windows 7?

(a) On the Start button, you can right-click the icon to view recently used files in a jump list.
(b) Link to folders containing the items you use the most.
(c) To easily access programs, you can attach or pin a program icon directly to the taskbar or Start menu.
(d) The command centre for configuring Windows settings.

5. A collection of web pages which are related to one another is called ________________ .

(a) Web Browser
(b) Home Page
(c) Website
(d) Search Engine

6. Which of the following would you use to shade a paragraph in MS Word 2010?

   (a)  (b) 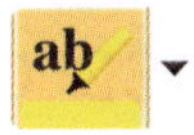 (c)  (d) 

7. Dynamic and Static are types of which type of memory?

   (a) ROM (b) CD-ROM (c) RAM (d) HDD

8. In the Windows 7 environment, the term used for Suspend to disk, Safe sleep or S4 modes is ________________ .

   (a) Sleep (c) Hibernate
   (b) Log off (d) Lock

9. A computer connected to a network is known as ________________ .

   (a) Workstation (c) Mainframe station
   (b) Network station (d) Server station

10. Which of the following is an advantage of computer network?

    (a) Share resources such as printer
    (b) Communicate with other users via videoconferencing
    (c) Share files
    (d) All of these

11. Bluetooth can be present in ________________ .

    (a) Keyboard (c) Digital cameras
    (b) Printers (d) All of these

12. Which of the following is the function of TV tuner card on your PC?

    (a) Enables computer to capture TV signals.
    (b) Enables computer to connect to the speakers on TV.
    (c) Lets you connect multiple monitors to the computer.
    (d) Clears the picture quality of your monitor.

13. Which of the following devices is required by voice recognition software in your computer?

    (a)  (c) 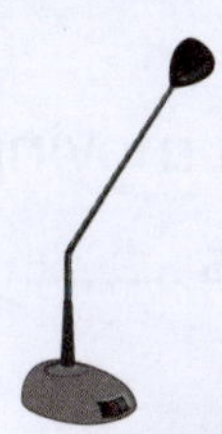

    (b)  (d) 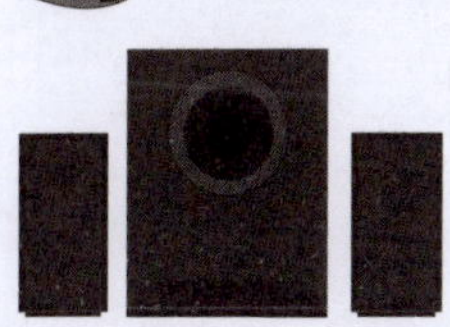

NATIONAL CYBER OLYMPIAD

14. Which of the following is NOT a type of a keyboard?
(a) QWERTY
(b) Concept
(c) Ergonomic
(d) ASDFG

15. An element on a web page like text or image that connects to the same or another document is known as ________________.
(a) Hyperlink
(b) Superlink
(c) URL
(d) None of these

16. Which of the following makes the use of a presentation software?
(a) Presenting sales performance to customers and clients
(b) Training employees in a company
(c) Teaching students in classrooms
(d) All of these

17. Which of the following is NOT present in View tab of MS PowerPoint 2010?
(a) Ruler (b) Grayscale (c) Hide Slide (d) Macros

18. In this MS PowerPoint 2010 view, all slides are arranged in miniature or thumbnail view on the screen.
(a) Reading view
(b) Slide Sorter view
(c) Slide Show view
(d) Normal view

19. How can you add an image from a file to your presentation in MS PowerPoint 2010?
(a) Select Insert tab → click picture command in images group
(b) Select Insert picture from file command in placeholder
(c) Both (a) and (b)
(d) Select Home tab → click picture command in images group

20. Which of the following is NOT a file format for music files?
(a) .wav
(b) .wma
(c) .mp3
(d) .avi

21. An illusionary effect of moving images created by displaying a series of pictures is known as ________________.
(a) Video
(b) Animation
(c) Audio
(d) Graphics

22. What is a major benefit of e-learning?
    (a) Students like using computers.
    (b) E-learning products are more informative than traditional learning resources.
    (c) Students can study at the time and place that suits them.
    (d) Computers are a better way of teaching than schools.

23. The given menu is present in ____________ tab of MS Word 2010 ribbon.

(a) Home (b) Insert (c) View (d) Page Layout

24. To make a picture double its actual size, which of the following tools will you use in MS Paint of Windows 7?

(a)  (b)  (c)  (d) 

25. A computer virus can ________________.
    (a) Delete data on your computer
    (b) Erase everything on hard disk
    (c) Spread through downloads from the Internet
    (d) All of these

26. Select the CORRECT match

(a)  – Video Card

(b)  – Power Supply

(c)  – Microprocessor

(d)  – Vacuum Tubes

27. The devices inside tablet PCs which detect the orientation of devices—as the user rotates the device the screen also changes its orientation.

(a) Digital device
(b) Sensors
(c) Scanners
(d) Rotating devices

28. Which of the following is the correct method of drawing an arc in MS Paint of Windows 7?
   (a) Selecting ∿ tool from Home tab in Tools group and dragging on the area.
   (b) Selecting ∿ tool from View tab in Tools group and dragging on the area.
   (c) Selecting ∿ tool from Home tab in Tools group and dragging on the area and drag the pointer on the line to make a curve.
   (d) Selecting \ tool from Home tab in Tools group.

29. I have three shapes numbered 1, 2 and 3. I want to put them together such that they can be moved together to any desired location on the document in MS Word 2010. First step is to use the Shift key combination to select them. What are the next steps?

   (a) Right-click on image ⟶ Select Grouping ⟶ Group
   (b) Double-click on image ⟶ Format tab opens ⟶ Select Group command from arrange group.
   (c) Either (a) or (b)
   (d) Right-click on image ⟶ Select Order ⟶ Group together

30. Identify the given MS PowerPoint 2010 icon.

   (a) Broadcast Slide Show
   (b) Custom Slide Show
   (c) Hide Slide
   (d) Rehearse Timings

WINDOWS 8

Windows 8 is an improved version of the Windows 7 operating system. It provides all of the basic features that Windows 7 has. The focus of Windows 8 is on optimizing the operating system for touchscreen-based devices (such as tablets) and cloud computing.

Unlike Windows Vista and Windows 7, there are no Starter, Home Basic, Home Premium or Ultimate editions in Windows 8. The most common editions of Windows 8 are Windows 8 Pro and Windows 8 Enterprise.

The new features specific to Windows 8 include the Start screen with semantic zoom, live tiles, Windows Store, Internet Explorer 10, connected standby, Microsoft account integration, the Windows desktop, etc. You can customize the looks of the Start screen according to your needs.

Fig. 1: Start-up screen of Windows 8

The interface also has a taskbar on the right side of the screen known as 'the charms', which can be accessed from any application or the desktop by sliding from the right edge of a touchscreen or compatible trackpad, moving the mouse cursor to one of the right corners of the screen, or pressing ⊞+C. The charms include Search, Share, Start, Devices and Settings charms. The Start charm begins or dismisses the Start screen.

Windows 8 introduces a new form of start menu called Start screen, which resembles the home screen of Windows Phone. The Start screen serves as the primary method of launching applications and is shown in place of the desktop on startup. The Start screen consists of a grid of tiles which can be arranged into columnar groups. The Start screen can uninstall applications directly.

Windows 8 does not have the Start button on the taskbar but it has other ways of beginning with the Start screen. Windows 8 also shows the Start screen on logon, unlike other versions of Windows which directly show the desktop.

Fig. 2: Locked screen of Windows 8

Windows 8 also has a new lock screen, which includes a date and time display, and a feature to display notifications from other applications. Two new login methods are also available for logging in to the system. You could either set a four-digit PIN or set a 'picture password'. This allows the user to use certain gestures performed on a selected picture to login. However, the shapes and gestures are limited to tapping and tracing a line or circle.

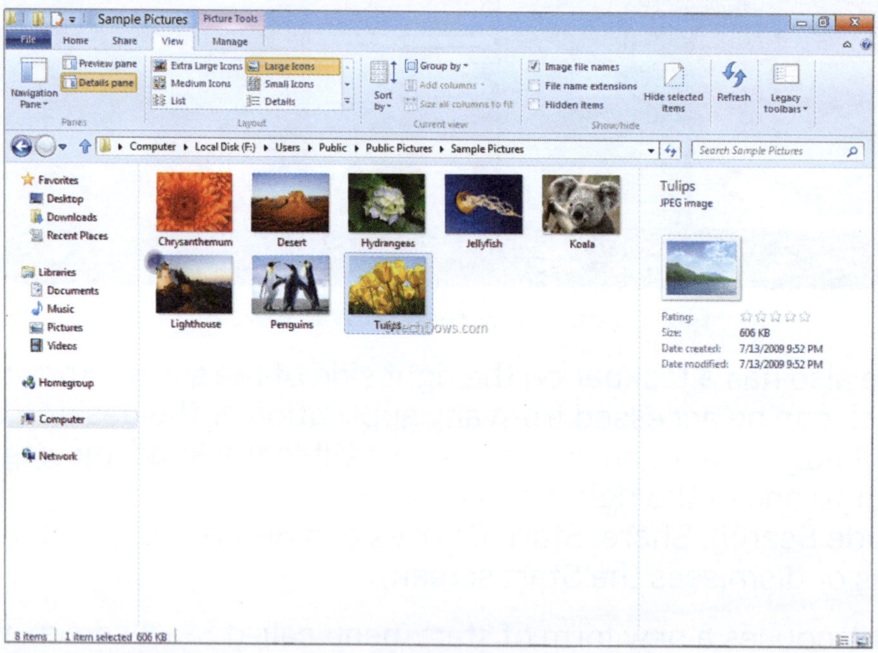

Fig. 3: File Explorer

Windows Explorer has been renamed as File Explorer. It has a ribbon toolbar which gives easy access to the most commonly used commands. The 'Up' button that used to take the user back a level in the folder hierarchy in previous versions of Windows has also been restored. Additionally, File Explorer features a redesigned preview pane that takes advantage of widescreen layouts.

MS WORD 2013

You all know that the **header** is a section of the document that appears in the top margin, while the **footer** is a section of the document that appears in the bottom margin. Headers and footers generally contain additional information such as page numbers, dates, an author's name, and footnotes, which can help keep longer documents organized and make them easier to read. Text entered in the header or footer appears on each page of the document.

To insert a header or footer:

Suppose, the user wants to add the author's name on the top of each page of a document; in this case header will be the best option.

1. Double-click anywhere on the **top or bottom margin** of your document. Here we have double-clicked on the top margin (Fig. 4).

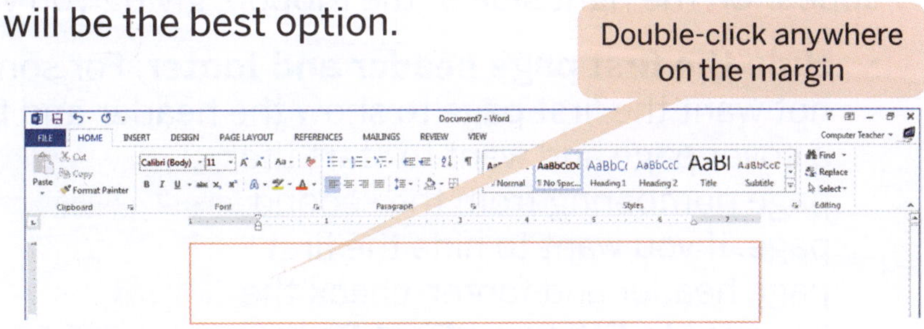

Fig. 4: Double-click in the top margin

2. The header or footer will open and a **Design** tab will appear on the right side of the **Ribbon**.

   The insertion point will appear in the header or footer (Fig. 5).

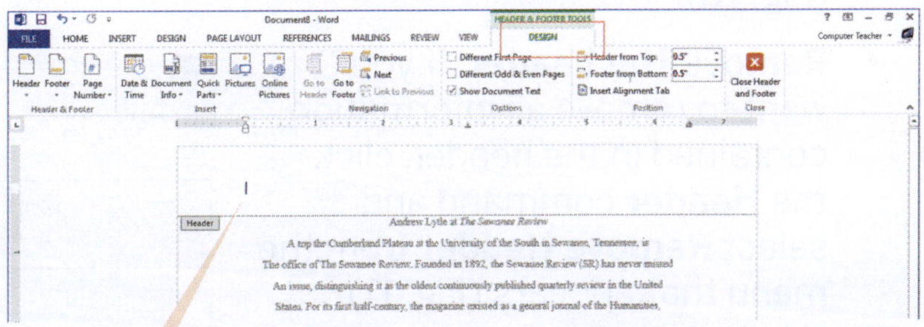

Fig. 5: Design tab on the Ribbon

3. Type the **desired information** into the header or footer.

   Here we have typed the author's name (Fig. 6).

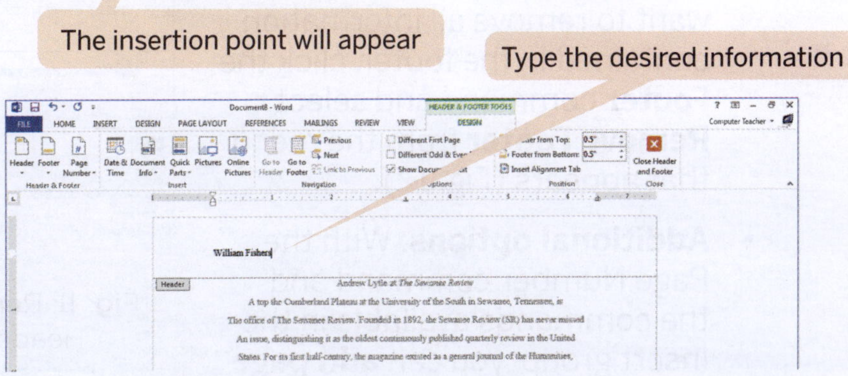

Fig. 6: Type the desired information

4. Once you have finished entering data in Header and Footer, click **Close Header and Footer** (Fig. 7). Alternatively, you can also press the **Esc** key.
5. The header or footer text will appear as shown in Fig. 8.

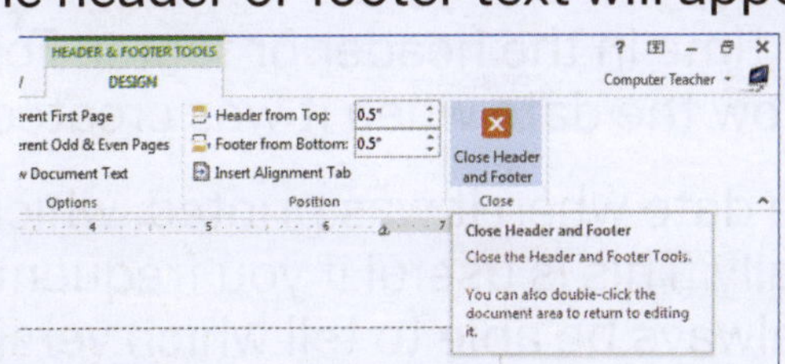

Fig. 7: Click Close Header and Footer

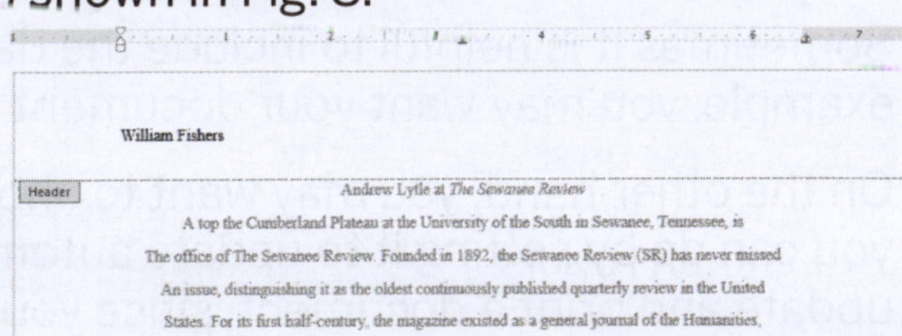

Fig. 8: Header text in the document

Editing headers and footers:

Even after you have closed the header or footer, it is still visible, but **locked** for editing. Simply double-click a header or footer to **unlock** it, which will allow you to edit its content (Fig. 9).

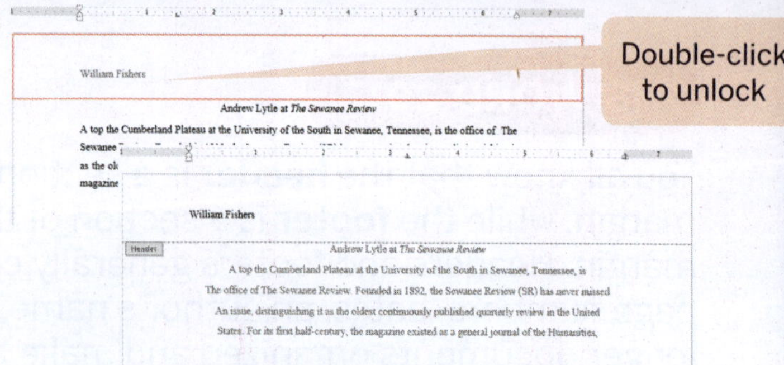

Fig. 9: Double-click on the header to unlock the header

Design Tab Options

When your document's header and footer are unlocked, the **Design** tab will appear on the right side of the Ribbon, giving you various editing options:

- **Hide the first page header and footer**: For some documents, you may not want the first page to show the header and footer, for example, you have a cover page and want to start the page numbering from the second page. If you want to hide the first page header and footer, check the box next to **Different First Page** (Fig. 10).

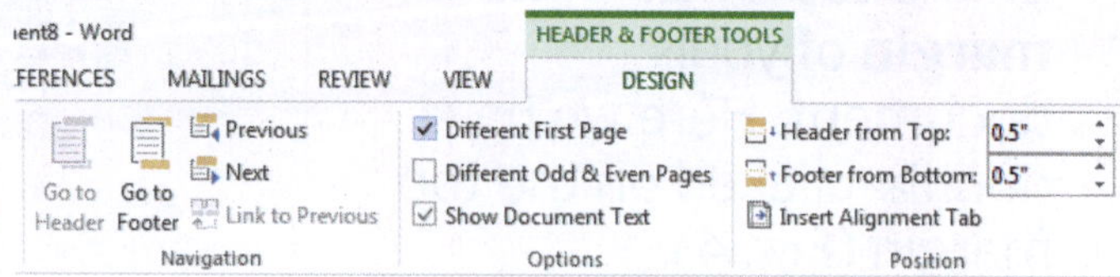

Fig. 10: Design tab options

- **Remove the header**: If you want to remove all information contained in the header, click the **Header** command and select **Remove Header** from the menu that appears (Fig. 11).
- **Remove the footer**: If you want to remove all information contained in the footer, click the **Footer** command and select **Remove Footer** from the menu that appears (Fig. 12).

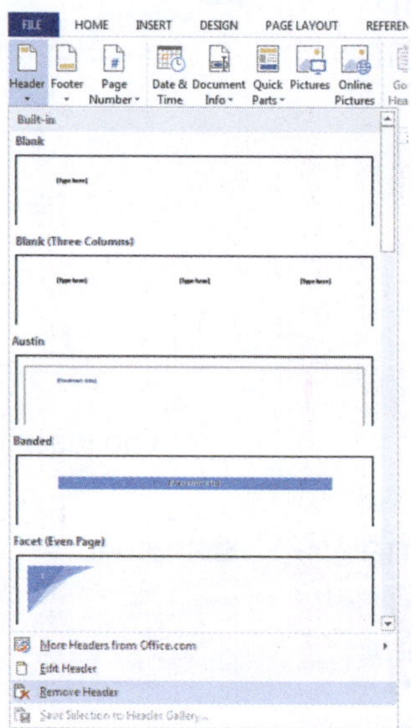

Fig. 11: Remove Header

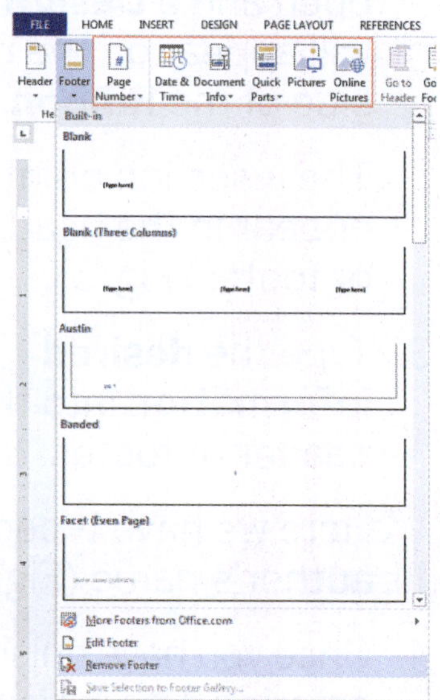

Fig. 12: Remove Footer

- **Additional options**: With the Page Number command and the commands available in the Insert group, you can **add page numbers**, the **date and time**, **pictures**, etc. to the header or footer.

To insert the date or time into a header or footer:

Sometimes it is helpful to include the date or time in the header or footer. For example, you may want your document to show the date when it was created.

On the other hand, you may want to show the date when it was printed, which you can do by setting it to update automatically. This is useful if you frequently update and print a document, since you will always be able to tell which version is the most recent.

1. Double-click anywhere on the header or footer to **unlock** it. Place the **insertion point** where you want the date or time to appear. Here, we have placed the insertion point on the line below the author's name (Fig. 13).

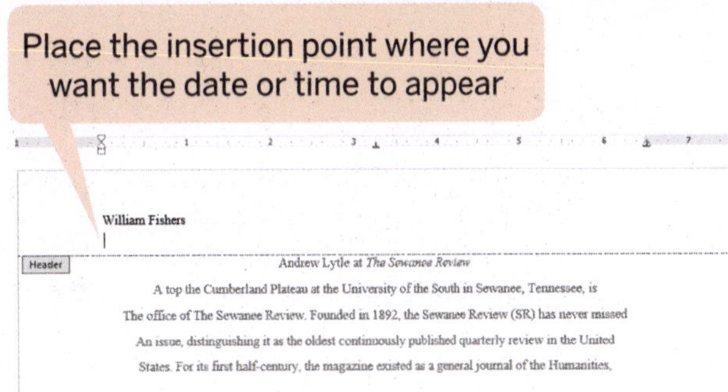

Fig. 13: Insertion point where the date and time are required

2. The **Design** tab will appear. Click the **Date & Time** command.
3. The **Date and Time** dialog box will appear. Select the desired **date** or **time format**.

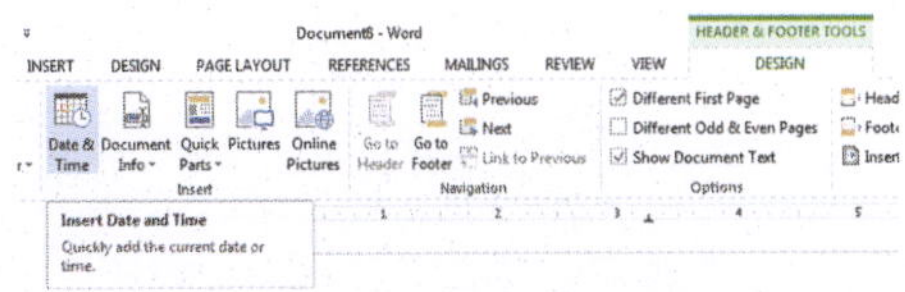

Fig. 14: Click on Date & Time

4. Check the box next to **Update Automatically** if you want the date to change every time you open the document. If you do not want the date to change, leave this option unchecked.
5. Click **OK**.
6. The date will appear in the header (Fig. 16).
7. Once you have inserted date and time, click **Close Header and Footer** (Fig. 17).

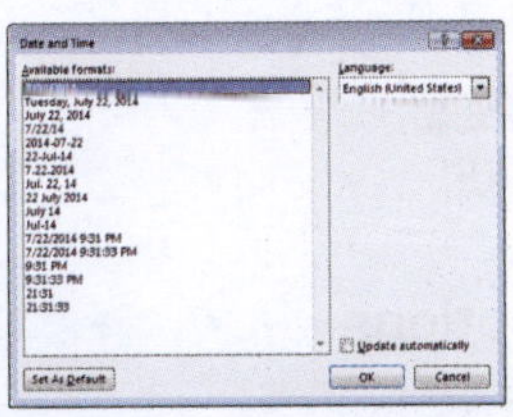

Fig. 15: Date and Time dialog box

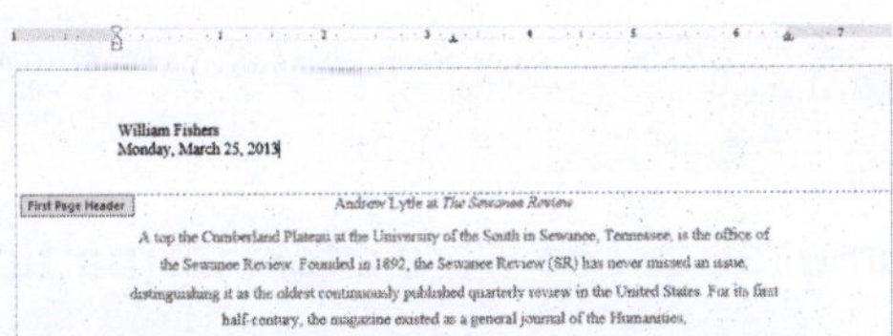

Fig. 16: Date appears at the insertion point

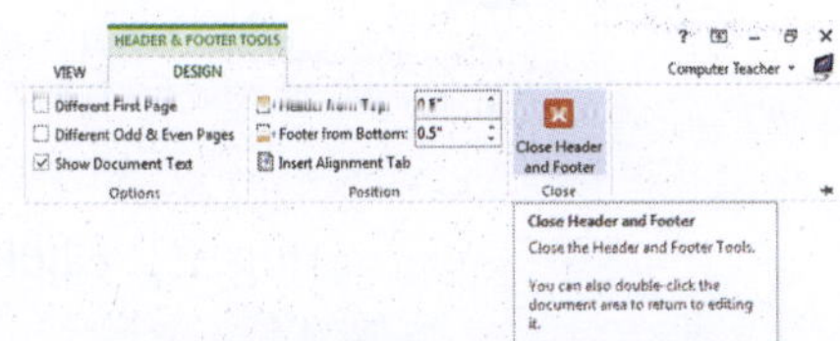

Fig. 17: Click Close Header and Footer

Adding Page Numbers

Word can automatically label each page with a page number and place it in a **header**, **footer**, or in the **side margin**. When you need to number some pages differently, Word allows you to **restart page numbering**.

To add page numbers to a document (shown for footer in this example)

1. Double-click anywhere on the **header** or **footer** to **unlock** it.

   If there are no header or footer in a document, you can double-click near the **top or bottom of the page**.

   The **Design** tab will appear on the right side of the Ribbon.

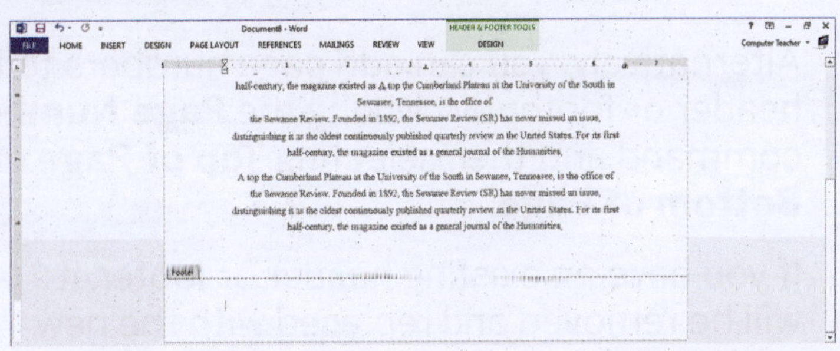

Fig. 18: Insertion Point where the page numbers are required

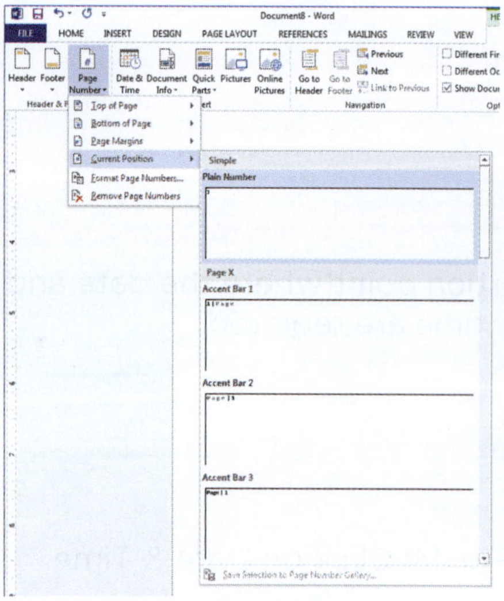

Fig. 19: Select the page numbering style

2. Click the **Page Number** command.

   In the menu that appears, hover the mouse over **Current Position** and select the desired **page numbering style** (Fig. 19).

3. Page numbering will appear (Fig. 20).

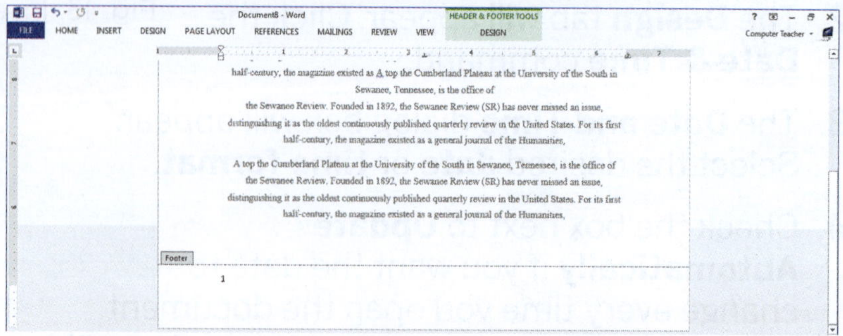

Fig. 20: Page number appears

2. To edit the **font**, **font size** and **alignment** of the page numbers, select a page number and click the **Home** tab. Word's text formatting options will appear as shown in Fig. 21.

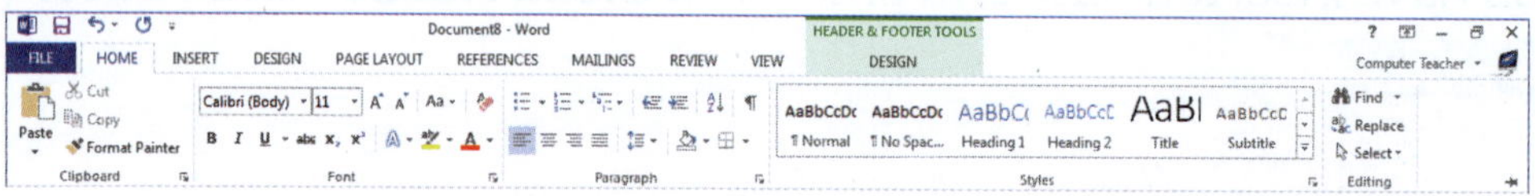

Fig. 21: Click Home tab to see Word's text formatting options

5. Once you are done, press the **Esc** key. The page numbering will be formatted (Fig. 22).

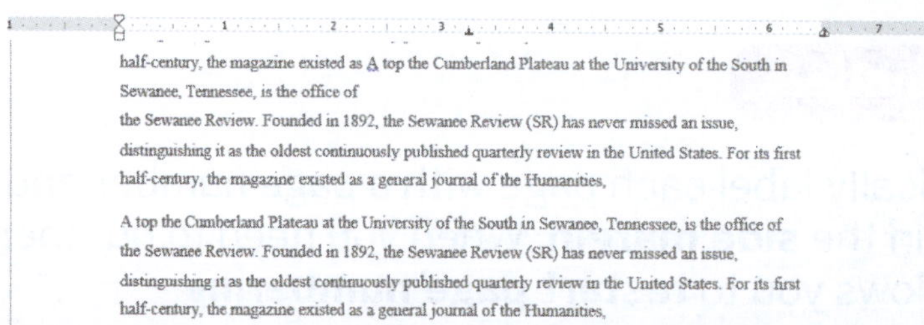

Fig. 22: Formatted page number in the document

Alternatively, you can add page numbers to the header or footer by clicking the **Page Number** command and then selecting **Top of Page** or **Bottom of Page**.

If you have an existing header or footer, it will be removed and replaced with the new page number.

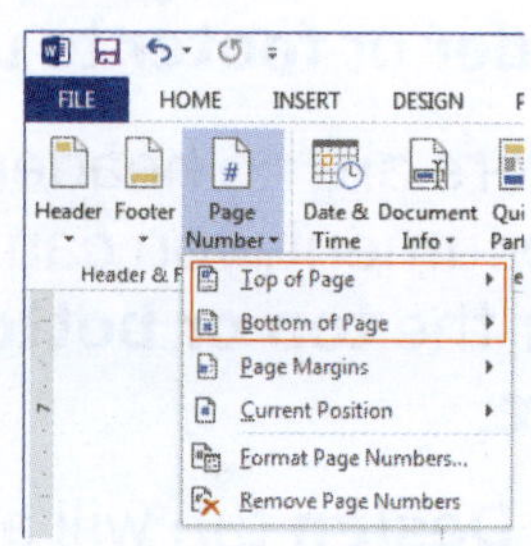

Fig. 23: Alternate method to add page numbers in the document

To restart page numbering:

Word allows you to restart page numbering on any page of the document. You can do this by inserting a section break and then selecting the number you like to restart the numbering with. Follow the steps given below to restart the page numbering.

1. Place the **insertion point** at the **top of the page** you want to restart page numbering for. If there is text on the page, place the insertion point at the **beginning of the text** (Fig. 24).

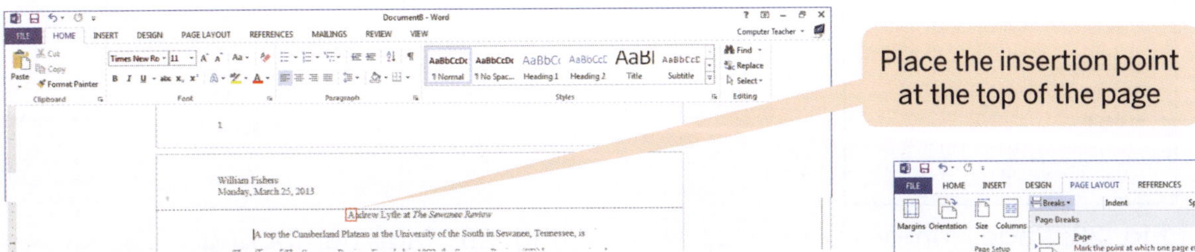

Fig. 24: Insertion Point from where the page numbering has to be restarted

2. Select the **Page Layout** tab and click the **Breaks** command.

   Select **Next Page** from the drop-down menu that appears (Fig. 25).

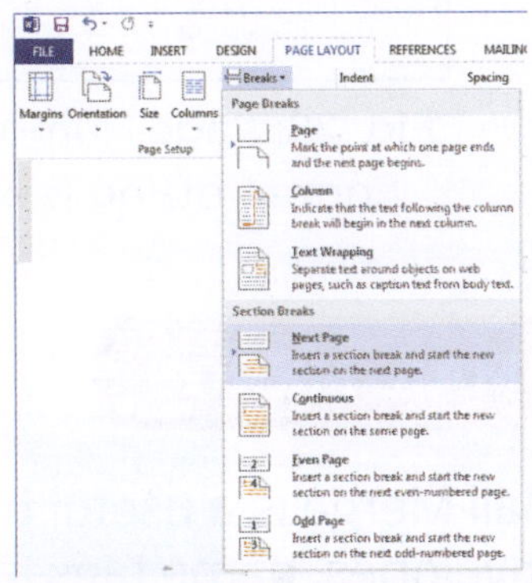

Fig. 25: Select Next Page from the Breaks drop-down menu

3. A section break will be added to the document.
4. Double-click the **header or footer** that contains the page number you want to restart (Fig. 26).

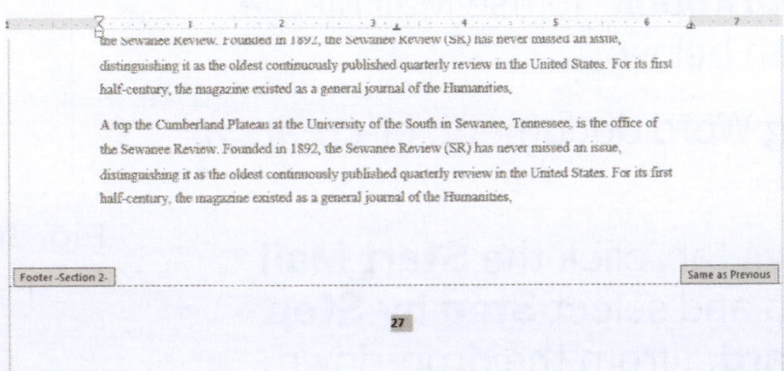

Fig. 26: Double-click the header/footer from where the renumbering has to be done

5. Click the **Page Number** command. In the menu that appears, select **Format Page Numbers** (Fig. 27).

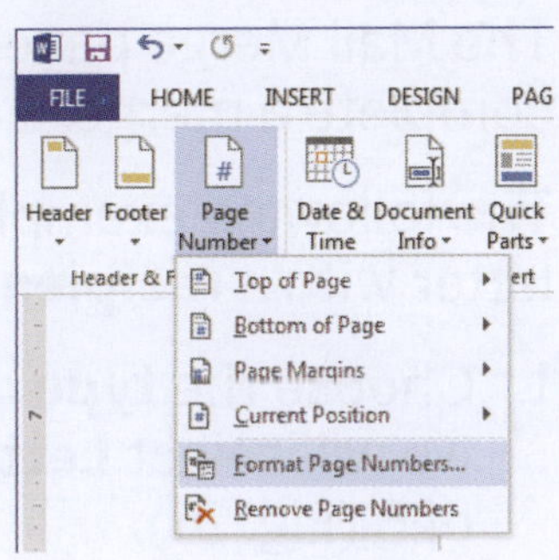

Fig. 27: Select Format Page Numbers

6. A dialog box will appear. Click the **Start at**: button (Fig. 28). By default, it will start at **1**. You can change this number as per your need.
7. Click **OK**.
8. The page numbering will restart (Fig. 29).

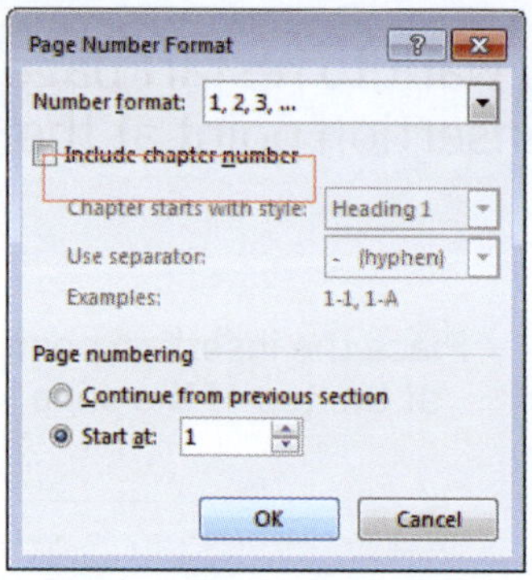

Fig. 28: Page Number Format dialog box

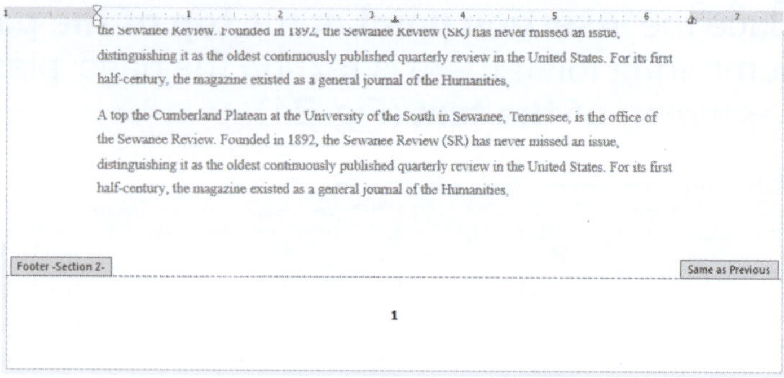

Fig. 29: Page numbering restarted from 1

MAIL MERGE

Mail Merge is a useful tool that allows you to produce multiple letters, labels, envelopes, name tags, and more using information stored in a list, database, or spreadsheet. When performing a **Mail Merge**, you will need a **Word document** (you can start with an existing one or create a new one) and a **recipient list**, which is typically an **Excel workbook**. To use Mail Merge, follow the steps given below:

1. Open an **existing** Word document, or create a **new** one.
2. From the **Mailings** tab, click the **Start Mail Merge** command and select **Step by Step Mail Merge Wizard...** from the drop-down menu (Fig. 30).

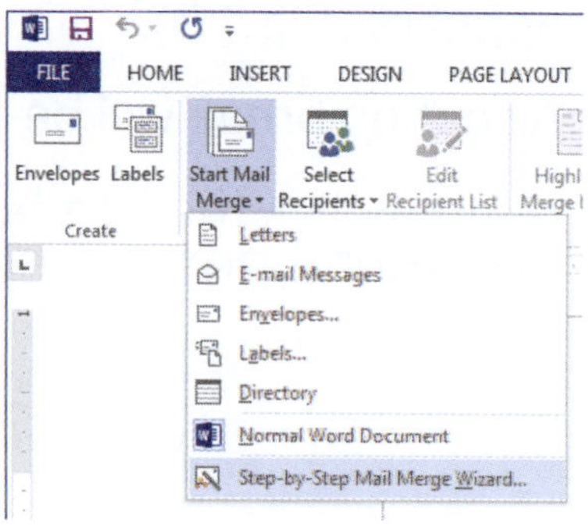

Fig. 30: Select Step by Step Mail Merge Wizard...

The Mail Merge pane appears and will guide you through the **main steps** to complete a merge.

The following example demonstrates how to create a form letter and merge the letter with a **recipient list**.

1. Choose the **type** of document you wish to create. In the example given below, we will select **Letters**. Then click **Next: Starting document** to move to Step 2 of 6 (Fig. 31).

2. Select **Use the current document**, then click **Next: Select recipients** to move to Step 3 of 6 (Fig. 32).
3. Now you will need an address list from where Word can automatically place each address into the document. The list can be in an existing file, such as an **Excel workbook**, or you can **type a new address list** from within the Mail Merge Wizard.

From the **Mail Merge** task pane, select **Use an existing list**, then click **Browse...** to select the file (Fig. 33).

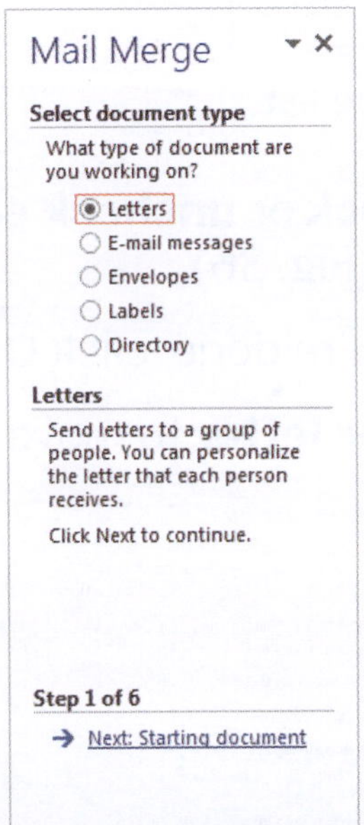

Fig. 31: Select Letters

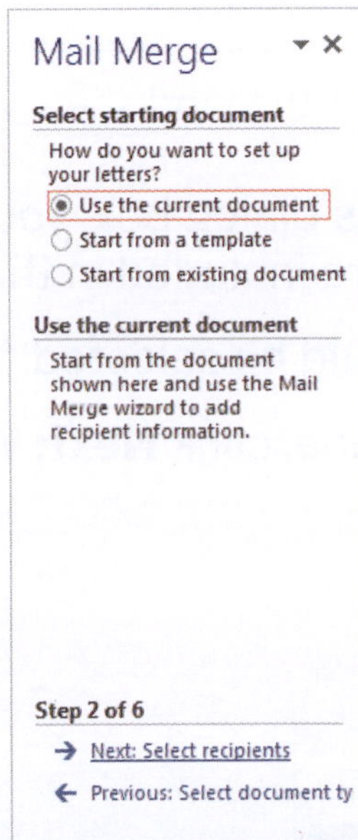

Fig. 32: Select Use the current document

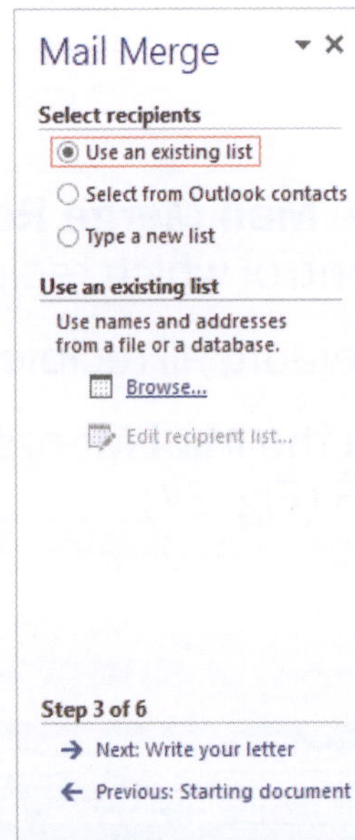

Fig. 33: Select Use an existing list

4. Locate your file and click **Open** (Fig. 34).

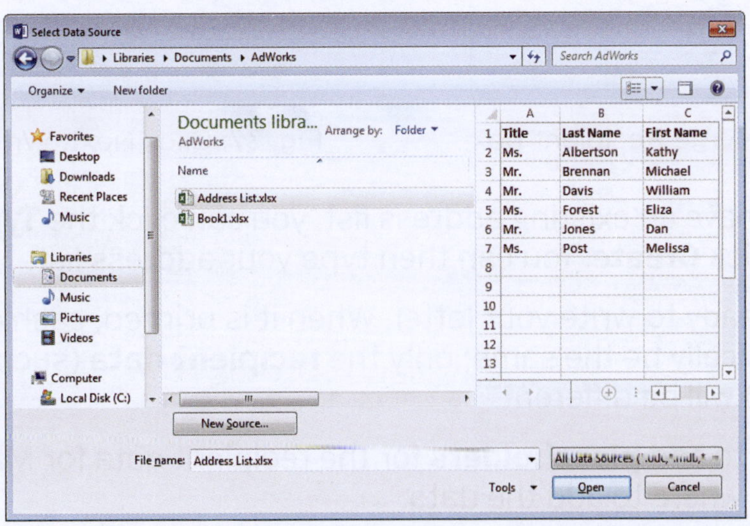

Fig. 34: Select Data Source dialog box

5. If the address list is in an Excel workbook, select the **worksheet** that contains the list and click **OK** (Fig. 35).

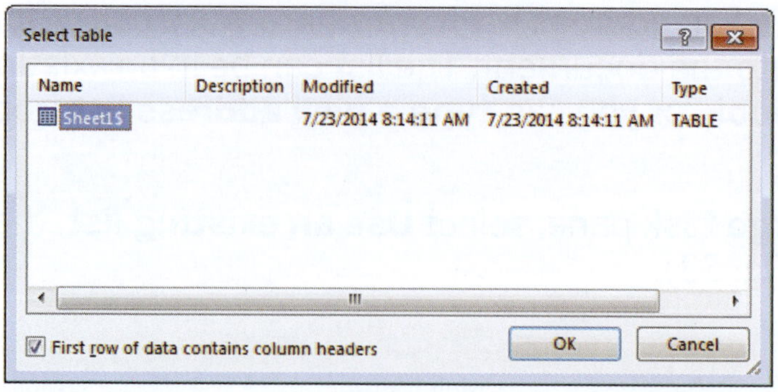

Fig. 35: Select the worksheet that has the list

6. In the **Mail Merge Recipients** dialog box, you can **check** or **uncheck** each box to control which recipients are included in the merge (Fig. 36).
7. By default, all recipients should be selected. When you're done, click **OK**.
8. From the **Mail Merge** task pane, click **Next: Write your letter** to move to Step 3 of 6 (Fig. 37).

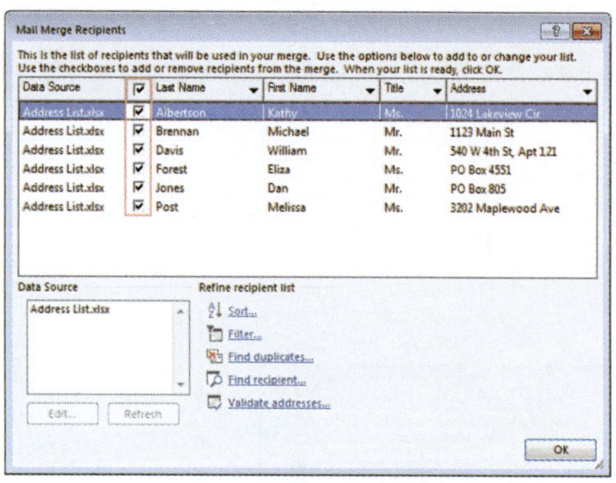

Fig. 36: Mail Merge Recipient box

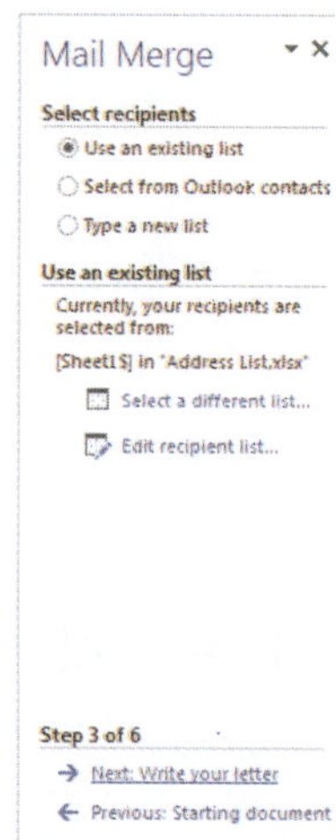

Fig. 37: Click Next: Write your letter

9. If you do not have an existing address list, you can click the **Type a new list** button and click **Create**. You can then type your address list.
10. Now you're ready to write your letter. When it is printed, each copy of the letter will basically be the same; only the **recipient data** (such as the **name** and **address**) will be different.

    You will need to add **placeholders** for the recipient data for Mail Merge to know exactly where to add the data.
11. To insert recipient data, place the insertion point in the document where you wish the information to appear.

12. Choose one of the four **placeholder** options: **Address block**, **Greeting line**, **Electronic postage**, or **More items** (Fig. 38).

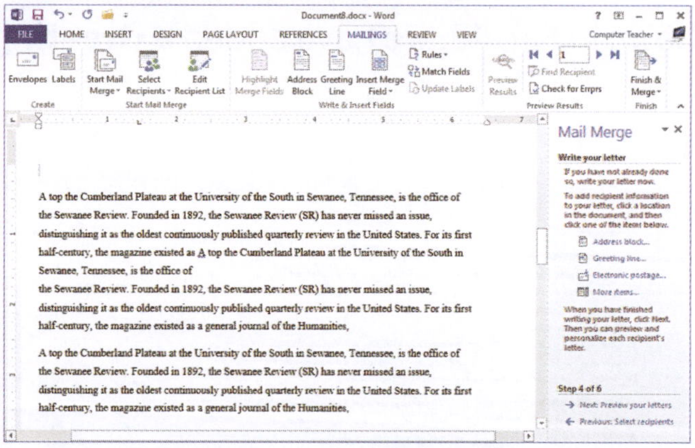

Fig. 38: Write the letter

13. Depending on your selection, a dialog box appears with various options (we have clicked Address Block in our example in Fig. 39). Select the desired options and click **OK** (Fig. 40).

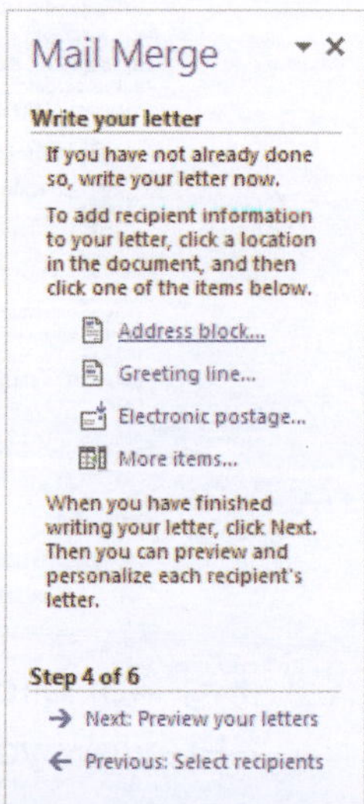

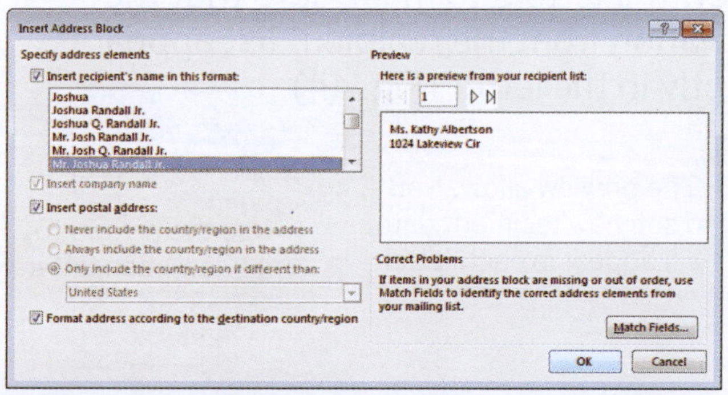

Fig. 39: Click on Address Block

Fig. 40: Insert Address Block dialog box

14. A placeholder will appear in your document. For example: **«AddressBlock»** (Fig. 41).

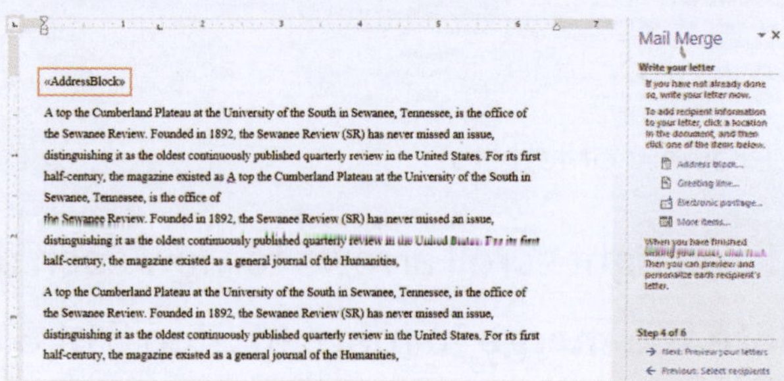

Fig. 41: Letter with a placeholder

15. Repeat these steps each time you need to enter information from your data record.

    In the example shown in Fig. 42, we have added a **Greeting line** also.

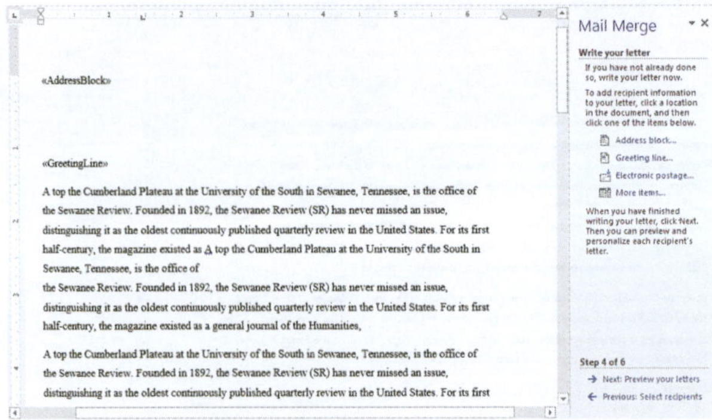

Fig. 42: Letter with two placeholders

16. When you 'are done, click **Next: Preview your letters** to move to Step 4 of 6 (Fig. 43).

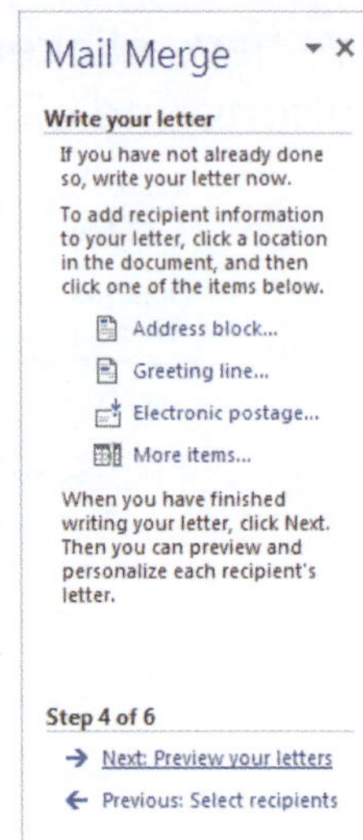

Fig. 43: Click on Next: Preview your letters

For some letters, you will only need to add an **Address block** and **Greeting line**. Sometimes, however, you may wish to place **recipient data** within the body of the letter to **personalize it** even further.

17. Preview the letters to make sure that the information from the recipient list appears correctly in the letter (Fig. 44).

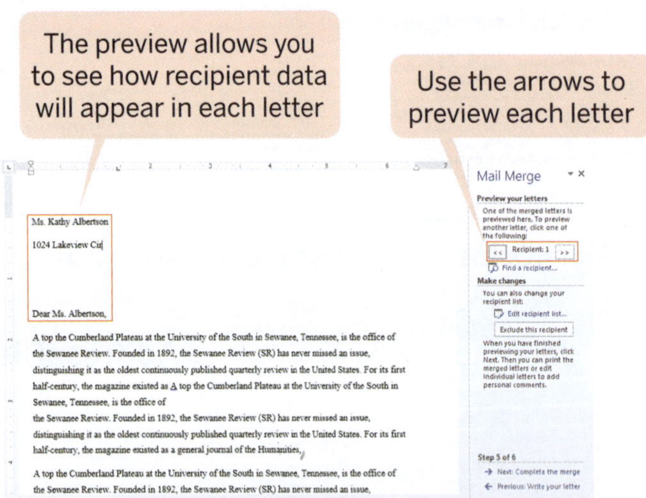

Fig. 44: Preview of letters

You can use the left and right scroll arrows to view each document.

18. Click **Next: Complete the merge** to move to Step 5 of 6 (Fig. 45).

19. Click **Print...** to print the letters to complete Step 6 of 6 (Fig. 46).

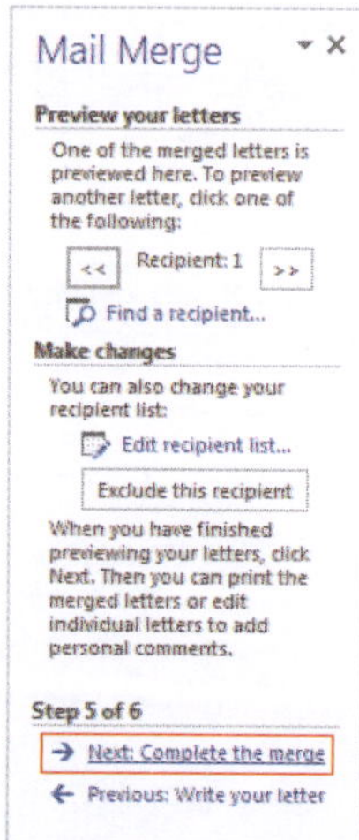

Fig. 45: Click Next: Complete the merge

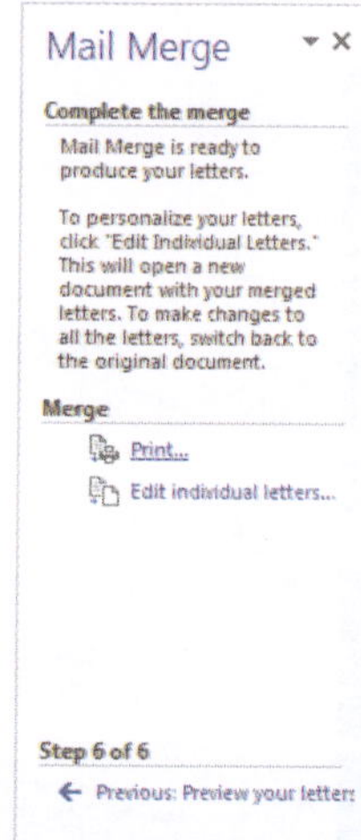

Fig. 46: Click Print

20. A dialog box will appear. Click **All**, then click **OK** (Fig. 47).
21. The **Print** dialog box will appear (Fig. 48). Adjust the print settings if needed, then click **OK**. The letters will be printed.

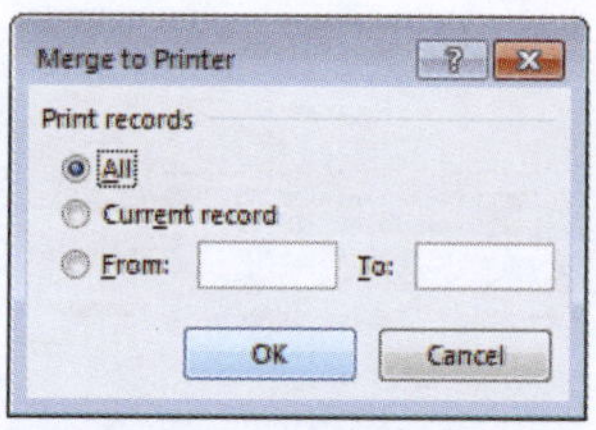

Fig. 47: Merge to Printer dialog box

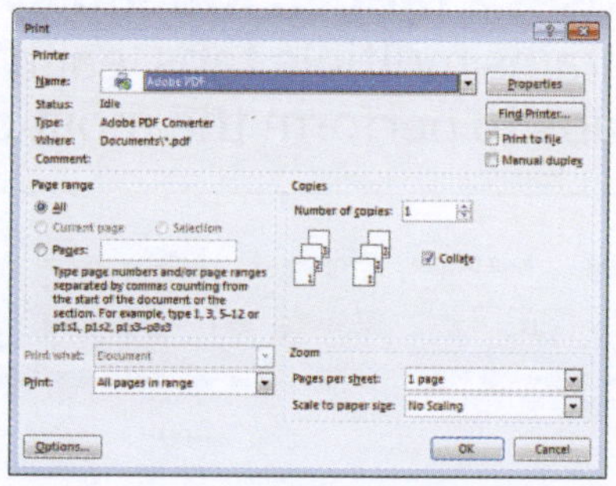

Fig. 48: Print dialog box

MS EXCEL 2013

Excel 2013 is a **spreadsheet program** that allows you to **store**, **organize** and **analyze information**. Excel is used not only by certain people to process complicated data, but anyone can learn how to take advantage of Excel's **powerful features**. Whether you are keeping a budget, organizing a training log, or creating an invoice, Excel makes it easy to work with different kinds of data.

The Excel Interface

When you open Excel 2013 for the first time, the **Excel Start Screen** will appear. From here, you will be able to create a **new workbook**, choose a **template** and access your **recently edited workbooks**.

- From the **Excel Start Screen**, locate and select **Blank workbook** to access the Excel interface (Fig. 49).

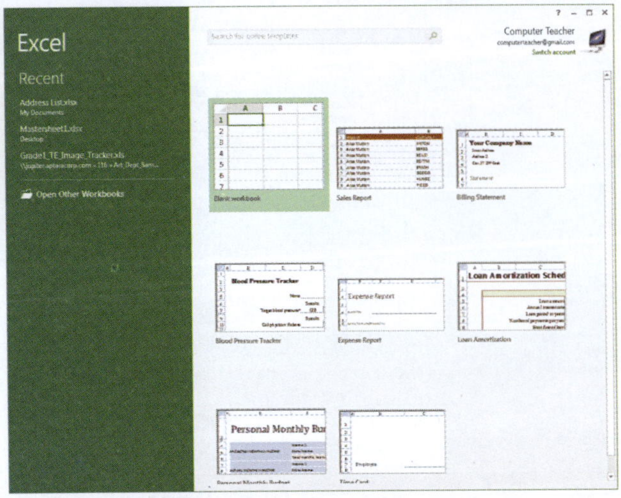

Fig. 49: Select Blank workbook

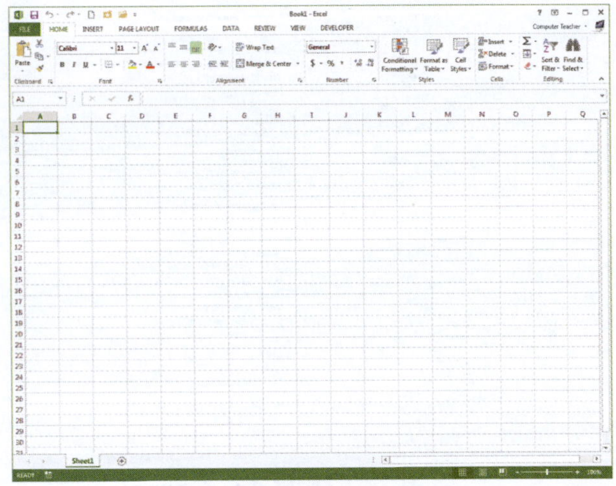

Fig. 50: New Workbook

The Ribbon

Excel 2013 uses a **tabbed Ribbon system** instead of traditional menus. The **Ribbon** contains multiple tabs, each with several groups of commands. You will use these tabs to perform the most common tasks in Excel.

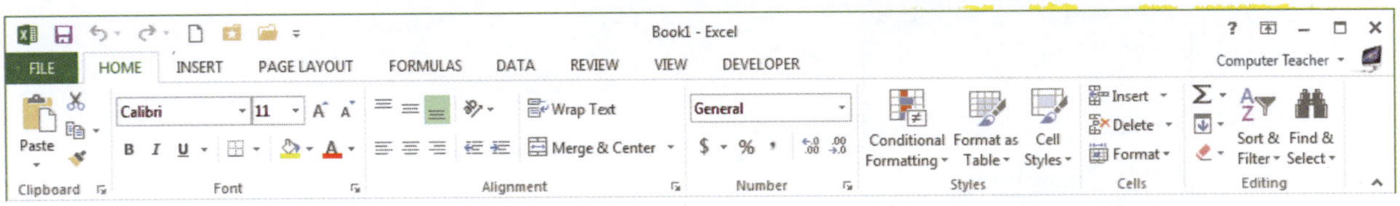

Fig. 51: Home tab

The **Home** tab gives you access to some of the most commonly used commands for working with data in Excel 2013, including **copy and paste**, **formatting** and **number styles**. The Home tab is selected by default whenever you open Excel (Fig. 51).

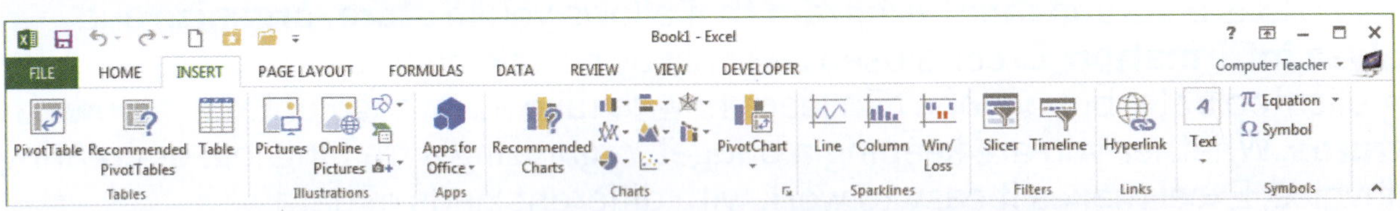

Fig. 52: Insert tab

The **Insert** tab allows you to insert **charts**, **tables**, **sparklines**, **filters**, and more, which can help you **visualize** and **communicate** your workbook data **graphically** (Fig. 52).

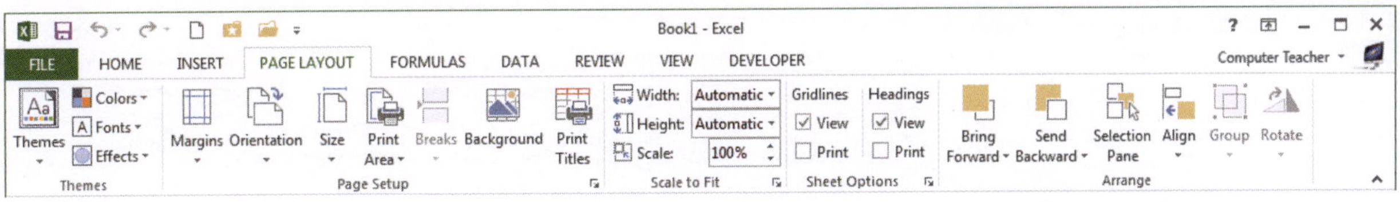

Fig. 53: Page Layout tab

The **Page Layout** tab allows you to change the **print formatting** of your workbook, including **margin width**, **page orientation**, and **themes**. These commands will be especially helpful when preparing to print a workbook (Fig. 53).

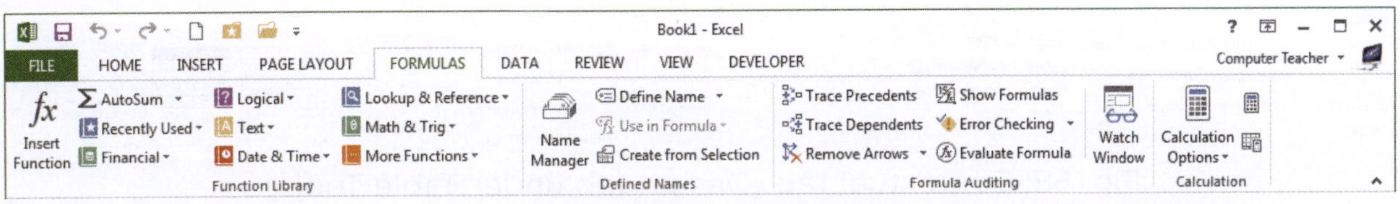

Fig. 54: Formulas tab

The **Formulas** tab gives you access to the most commonly used **functions** and **formulas** in Excel. These commands will help you **calculate** and **analyze numerical data**, like averages and percentages (Fig. 54).

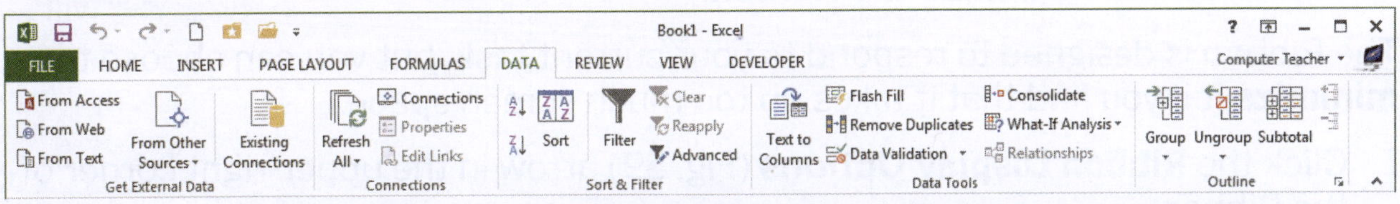

Fig. 55: Data tab

The **Data** tab makes it easy to **sort** and **filter** information in your workbook, which can be especially helpful if your project contains a **large amount** of data (Fig. 55).

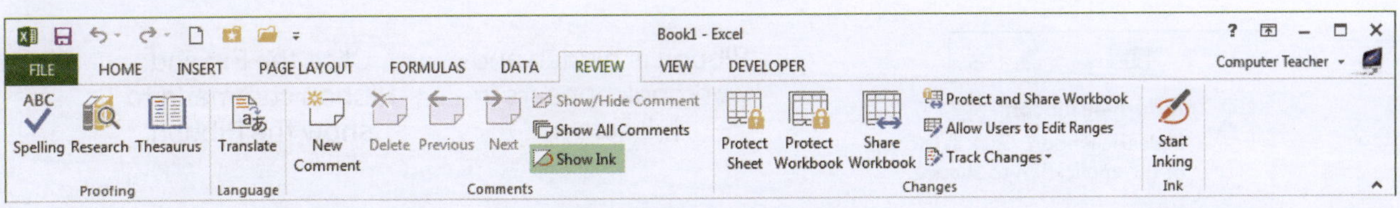

Fig. 56: Review tab

You can use the **Review** tab to access Excel's powerful **editing features**, including **comments** and track **changes**. These features make it easy to **share** and **collaborate** on workbooks (Fig. 56).

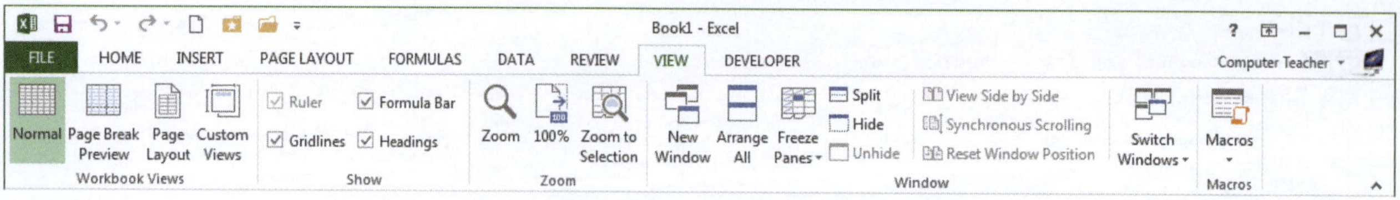

Fig. 57: View tab

The **View** tab allows you to switch between different **views** for your workbook and **freeze panes** for easy viewing. These commands will also be helpful when preparing to print a workbook (Fig. 57).

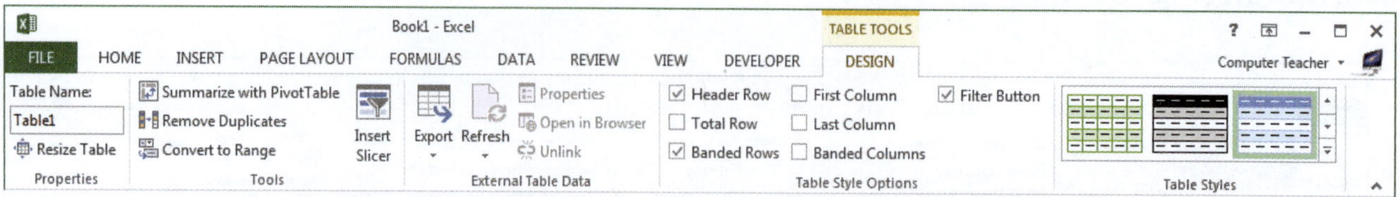

Fig. 58: Contextual tab (Design tab under Table Tools)

Contextual tabs will appear on the Ribbon when working with certain items, like **tables** and **pictures**. These tabs contain special command groups that can help you format these items as needed (Fig. 58).

To minimize and maximize the Ribbon:

The Ribbon is designed to respond to your current task, but you can choose to **minimize** it if you find that it takes up too much screen space.

1. Click the **Ribbon Display Options** (Fig. 59) arrow in the upper-right corner of the Ribbon.
2. Select the desired **minimizing option** from the drop-down menu:
   - **Auto-hide Ribbon**: Auto-hide displays your workbook in full-screen mode and completely hides the Ribbon (Fig. 60). To **show the Ribbon**, click the **Expand Ribbon** command at the top of screen.

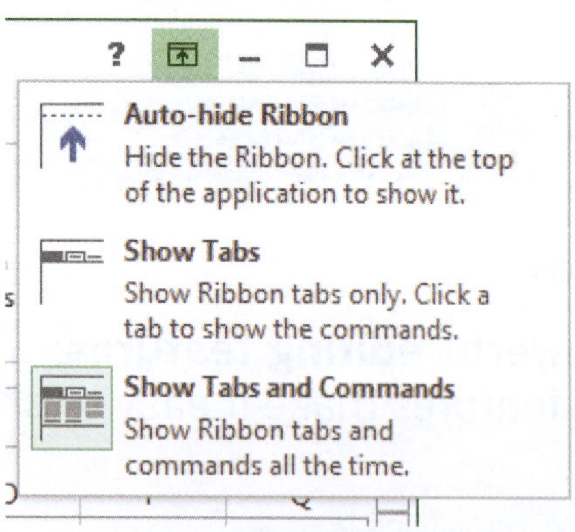

Fig. 59: Click Ribbon Display Options

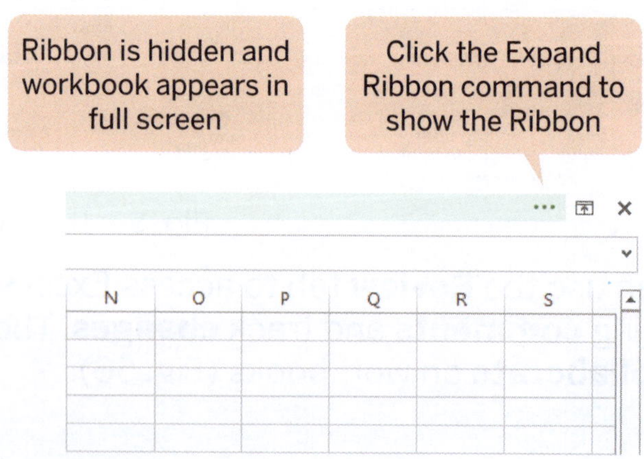

Fig. 60: Worksheet with hidden Ribbon

- **Show Tabs**: This option hides all command groups when not in use, but **tabs** will remain visible. To **show the Ribbon**, simply click a tab (Fig. 61).
- **Show Tabs and Commands**: This option maximizes the Ribbon. All of the tabs and commands will be visible. This option is selected by default when you open Excel for the first time.

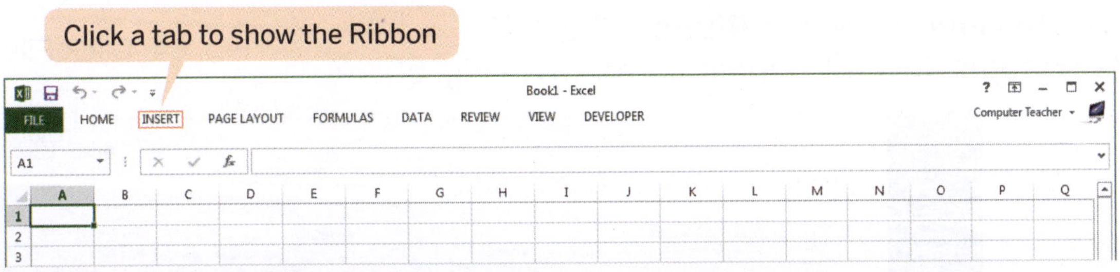

Fig. 61: Click a tab to show the Ribbon

The Quick Access Toolbar

Located just above the Ribbon, the **Quick Access Toolbar** lets you access common commands no matter which tab is selected. By default, it includes the **Save**, **Undo**, and **Repeat** commands. You can add other commands depending on your preference.

To add commands to the Quick Access Toolbar:

1. Click the **drop-down arrow** to the right of the **Quick Access Toolbar**.
2. Select the **command** you wish to add from the drop-down menu. To choose from more commands, select **More Commands** (Fig. 62).
3. The command will be **added** to the Quick Access Toolbar (Fig. 63).

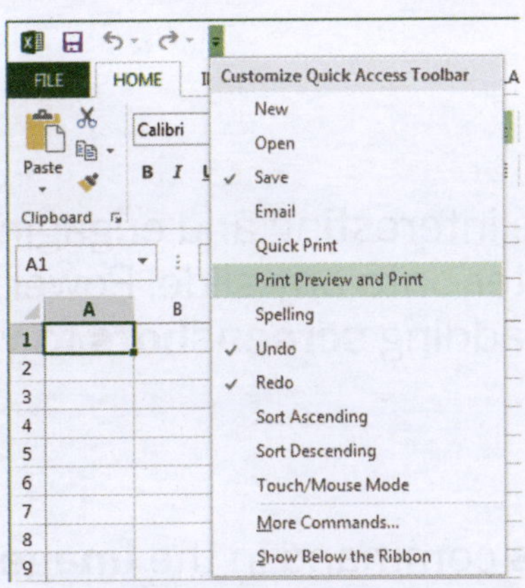

Fig. 62: Customizing the Quick Access Toolbar

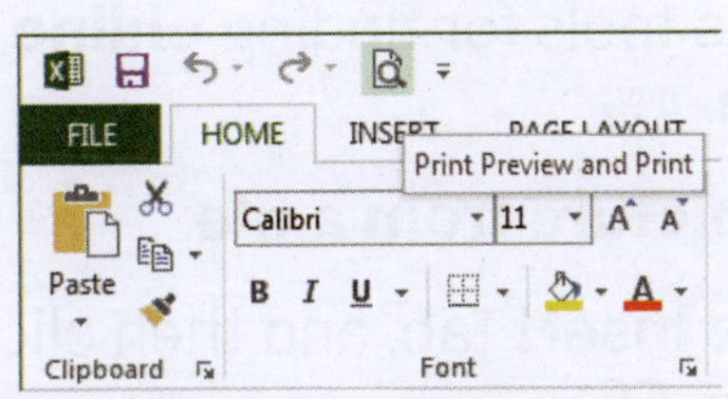

Fig. 63: Quick Access Toolbar with new options added

Backstage View

Backstage view gives you various options for saving, opening a file, printing, or sharing your workbooks.

To access Backstage view:

1. Click the **File** tab on the **Ribbon** (Fig. 64). **Backstage view** will appear as shown in Fig. 65.

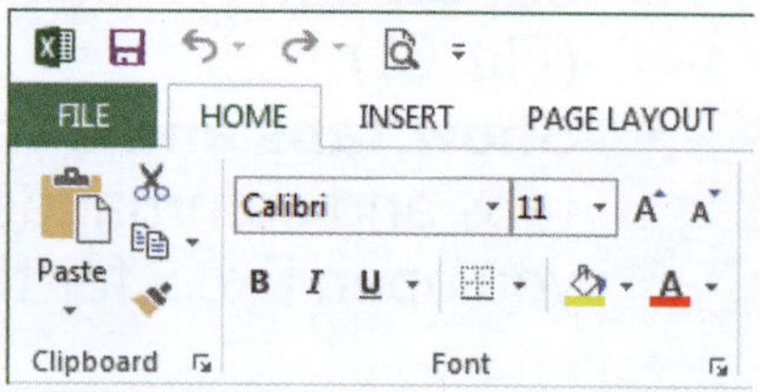

Fig. 64: Click File tab

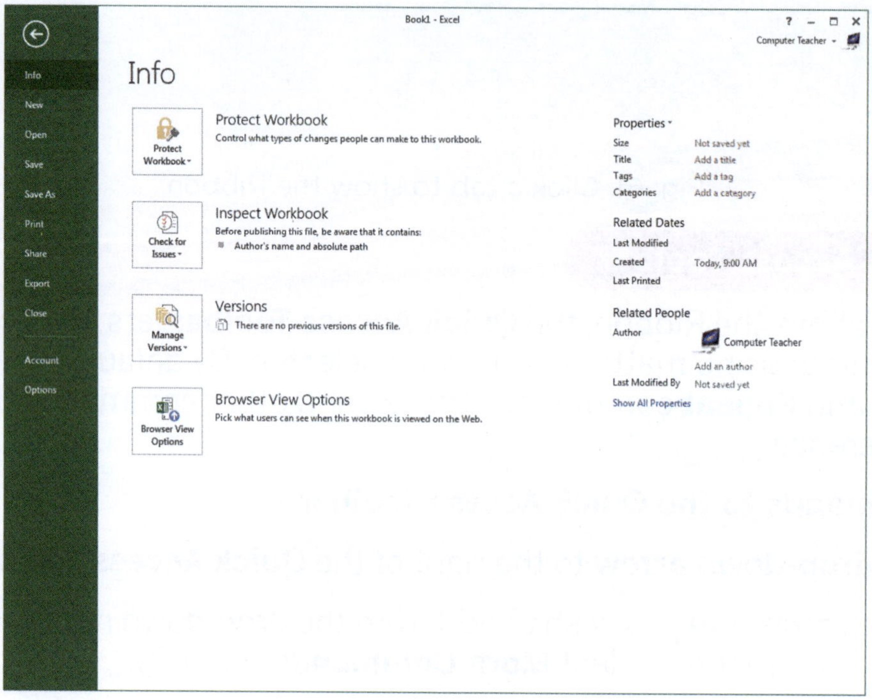

Fig. 65: Backstage view

MS POWERPOINT 2013

Adding **pictures** can make your presentations more interesting and engaging. You can insert a **picture from a file** on your computer onto any slide. PowerPoint even includes tools for finding **online pictures** and adding **screenshots** to your presentation.

To insert a picture from a file:

1. Select the **Insert** tab, and then click the **Pictures** command in the **Images** group (Fig. 66).

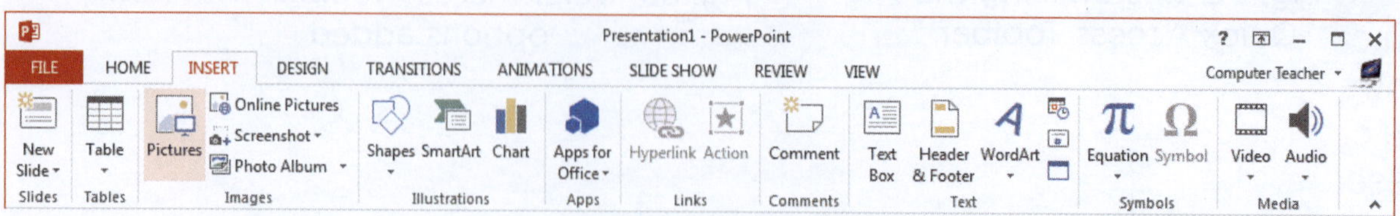

Fig. 66: Click on Pictures

2. A dialog box will appear (Fig. 67). Locate and select the **desired image file**, then click **Insert**.

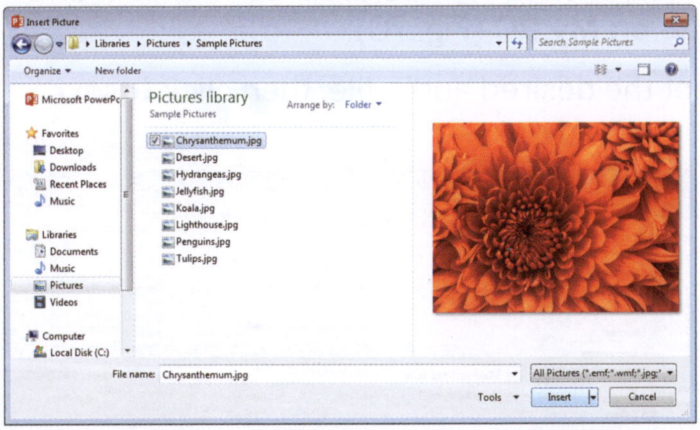

Fig. 67: Insert Picture dialog box

3. The picture will appear on the currently selected slide (Fig. 68).

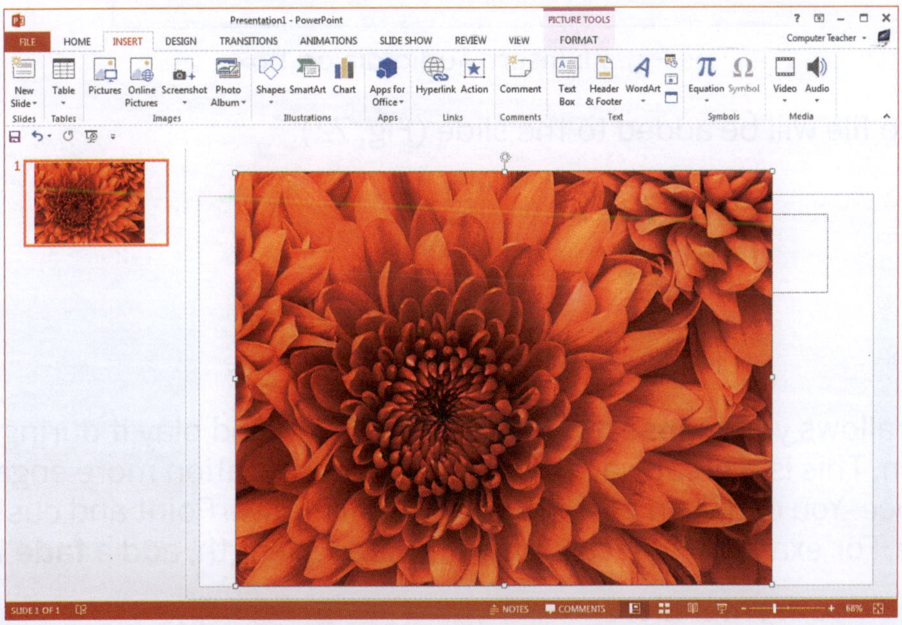

Fig. 68: Slide with the inserted picture

You can also click the **Pictures** command in a **placeholder** to insert images (Fig. 69).

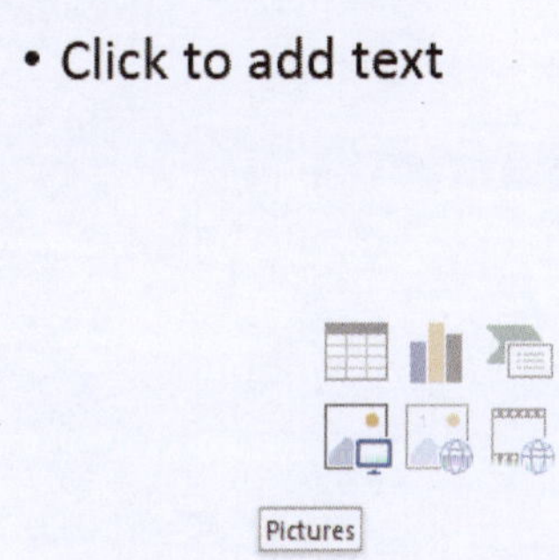

Fig. 69: Placeholder with Pictures command

PowerPoint allows you to add **audio** to your presentation. For example, you could add **background music** to one slide, a **sound effect** to another, and even record your own **narration** or **commentary**.

You can add sound **from a file** on your computer or browse PowerPoint's collection of **clip art audio**. You can then **edit** the audio to customize it for your presentation.

To insert audio from a file:

1. From the **Insert** tab, click the **Audio** drop-down arrow, and then select **Audio on My PC** (Fig. 70).

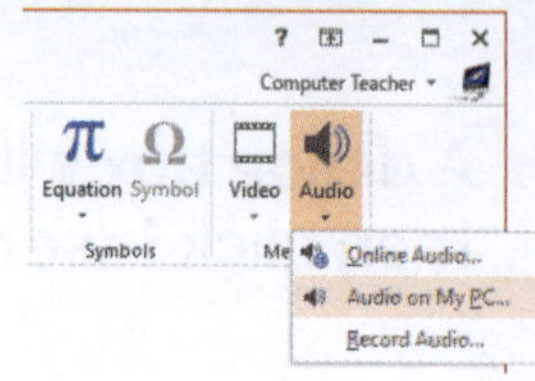

Fig. 70: Click Audio on My PC

2. Locate and select the desired audio file, then click **Insert** (Fig. 71).

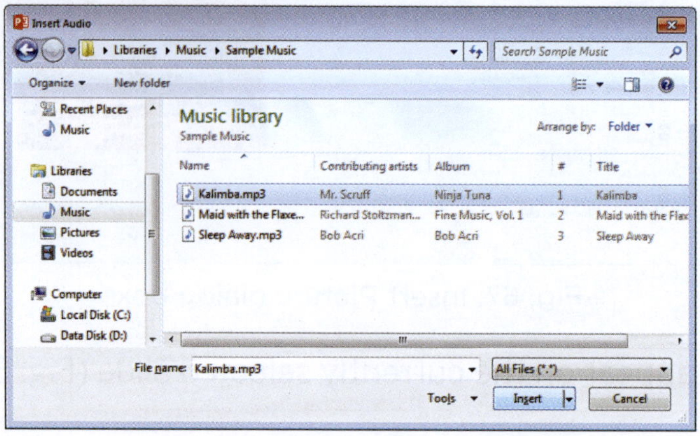

Fig. 71: Insert Audio dialog box

3. The audio file will be added to the slide (Fig. 72).

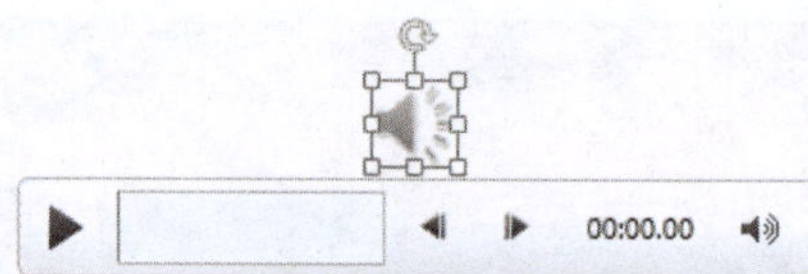

Fig. 72: Audio added to the slide

PowerPoint allows you to **insert a video** onto a slide and play it during your presentation. This is a great way to make your presentation more engaging for your audience. You can even **edit** the video within PowerPoint and customize its appearance. For example, you can **trim** the video's length, add a **fade in**, etc.

To insert a video from a file:

1. From the **Insert** tab, click the **Video** drop-down arrow, then select **Video on My PC** (Fig. 73).

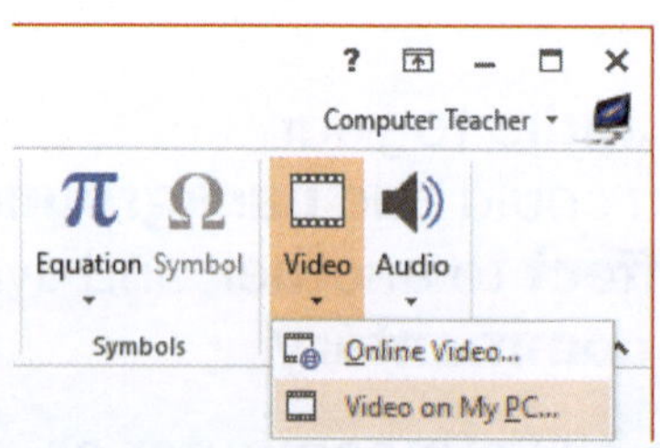

Fig. 73: Click Video on My PC

2. Locate and select the desired video file, then click **Insert** (Fig. 74).

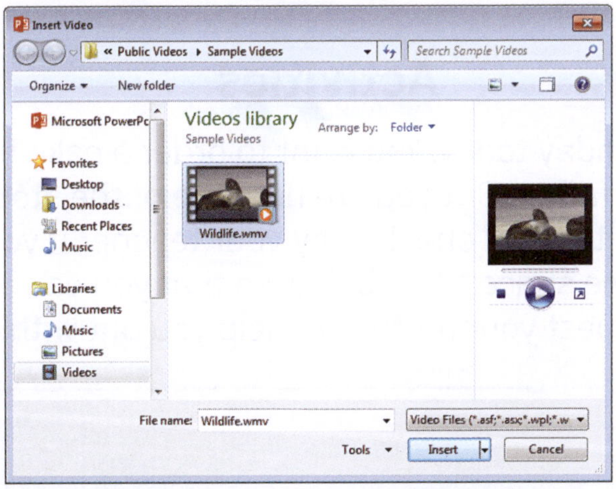

Fig. 74: Insert Video dialog box

3. The video will be added to the slide (Fig. 75).

Fig. 75: Video added to the slide

Activities

1. It is your father's birthday today. You want to order a cake from your favourite bakery shop for your father. But you are not sure of the steps of how to order and, hence, you want to get it checked by your teacher if you are right or not. Draw a flowchart in the space given below so that you can show it to your teacher and then request your mother to help you out with the payment.

2. Your English teacher has asked you to prepare a chart on various tenses. Search the Internet, grammar books and reference material from the library to prepare the same. Draw a flowchart to show the steps you followed to complete this task.

3. Draw a flowchart for the steps that you should follow while crossing the road. Also, mention the safety rules that one must follow as a pedestrian.

4. Write the MSWLogo commands that you would follow to draw the structural outline of the Indian flag. Also, draw the same in the space provided.

5. Write the MSWLogo commands to draw the roadmap for reaching your school from your home. Also, draw the output that you would get in the space given below and see if you were correct in drawing the roadmap.

6. Write the MSWLogo commands to draw a pattern of rangoli that you would like to make on the auspicious occasion of Diwali. Also, draw the output that you would get in the space given below.

7. Write a letter that you would like to send to five of your friends for inviting them to a Christmas party organized by your parents at your home. Mark the data (fields/placeholders) that you would like to pick from a data source while you write the letter in the space given below. Now, use this letter to create your main document while using the Mail Merge feature.

8. How would you feel while moving from the primary wing of your school to the middle school wing? Pen down your thoughts in the space given below so that the same can be used to create a blog of your feelings.

Notes